CHINA'S GUINNESS WORLD RECORDS

GUINNESS WORLD RECORDS™

中国的吉尼斯世界纪录

海豚出版社
DOLPHIN BOOKS
中国国际出版集团

图书再版编目（CIP）数据

中国的吉尼斯世界纪录：英汉对照 ／ 吴晓红主编，BEN WAY（英国）执行主编；
－北京：海豚出版社 ,2010.5

书名原文：China's Guinness World Records
ISBN 978－7－80138－795－0

Ⅰ.①中… Ⅱ.①吴… ② （英）B…Ⅲ.①科学知识－普及读物 Ⅳ . ① Z228

中国版本图书馆 CIP 数据核字（2010）第 064644 号

总策划：俞晓群

书　　名：CHINA'S GUINNESS WORLD RECORDS 中国的吉尼斯世界纪录

主　　编：吴晓红　　　　　　　　　　　　　出版发行：海豚出版社
执行主编：BEN WAY（英国）　　　　　　　电　　话：010－68997480（销售）
责任编辑：吕　莺　于婉青　赵智熙　李忠孝　传　　真：010－68998879
设计制作：北京大盟文化艺术有限公司　　　经　　销：新华书店
美术指导：李　萌　　　　　　　　　　　　开　　本：635mm×965mm　1/8
美术编辑：毛志强　徐小溪　柴　枫　　　　版　　次：2010 年 6 月第 1 版
印　　张：11　　　　　　　　　　　　　　印　　次：2010 年 6 月第 1 次印刷
印　　刷：北京华联印刷有限公司　　　　　书　　号：ISBN 978－7－80138－795－0
监　　印：曲克明　于浩杰　　　　　　　　　　　　　027900

CHINA'S
GUINNESS
W★RLD
RECORDS

中国的吉尼斯世界纪录

目录
Contents

Preface

The certificate presenting ceremony of "the largest one day golf tournament".

吉尼斯世界纪录为"参赛人员最多的高尔夫球比赛活动"颁发证书。↑

Guinness World Records has been a publisher of annual bestselling titles for over half a century. Since publishing the first edition of our annual bestselling title – the Guinness World Records book – in 1955, we have sold over 115 million books worldwide, making it a Guinness World Records holder in its own right: the bestselling copyright title of all time.

THE STORY OF GUINNESS

The 55-year history of Guinness World Records began with a single question, the type of question that has been repeated millions of times at restaurants, kitchen tables, classrooms and work places across the globe.

During a shooting party in County Wexford, Ireland, in 1951, Sir Hugh Beaver – then Managing Director of the Guinness Brewery – asked a simple question: what was Europe's fastest game bird? Despite a heated argument and an exhaustive search within the host's reference library he could not find the answer.

The adjudicator Wu Xiaohong from Guinness World Records is presenting the certificate to the organizer of the attempt of "the largest fruit mosaic".

吉尼斯世界纪录认证官吴晓红为"最大的水果拼图活动"主办方颁发证书。↑

Sir Hugh realized that similar questions were going unanswered all around the world, and that a definitive book containing superlative facts and answers would be of great use to the general public. With the help of the London-based fact-finding twins Norris and Ross McWhirter, he soon set about bringing this definitive collection of superlative facts to reality. On 27 August 1955, the first edition of "The Guinness Book of Records" was bound and, by Christmas that year, became Britain's number one bestseller.

Today, the Guinness World Records book is a publishing phenomenon, sold in 26 languages,

The students and teachers were very happy after they achieved the record for "the largest painting by numbers".

创造 "最大填色画" 吉尼斯世界纪录的部分学生及老师。 ↑

Guinness World Records adjudicator Marco Frigatti is adjudicating the attempt of "the heaviest shoes walked in" by a Chinese person.

吉尼斯世界纪录认证官马可·弗里加迪、主持人朱迅在认证 "穿最重的鞋行走" 的纪录现场。 ↑

in more than 100 countries worldwide, selling over 3.5 million books annually in the process. Each year, Guinness World Records explodes into book retailers across the globe on the back of an international PR campaign.

GUINNESS WORLD RECORDS IN CHINA

The first Chinese version of Guinness World Records was published in Liaoning province in 2000, followed by reprints that gained further popularity across the country. Since 2006, China Central Television has been working with Guinness World Record to produce series of television shows based on record breaking. Due to the successful internationalization of the show and the excellent presentations of the famous hosts and hostesses, *Zheng Da Zong Yi-Guinness World Records Special* has been bringing exciting experiences to audiences in China and other countries.

Dolphin Books from the China International Publishing Group has the authorization from Guinness World Records to produce a book dedicated to the records set by China –

China's Guinness World Records. Unlike the usual Guinness World Records publication, which showcase records from all countries in the world, this book contains only records set by China, in order to show the rapid progress of China from the perspective of Guinness World Records.

China's Guinness World Records is rich in content. This book reveals the excellences of China through the words and pictures contained in it, with records such as the largest palace, tallest building, highest railway line, oldest opera singer, for example. The book also includes the culture of the ancient times in China, such as earliest written language, earliest seismograph and the longest ancient city wall, to name just a few.

Welcome to the amazing world of Guinness World Records in China! Get ready to be astounded and inspired by the Chinese people who have recorded their names in history and the ancient people who created the wonderful treasures.

If you would like to apply for a record, please visit the website of Guinness World Records at www.guinnessworldrecords.com.

Presenter Zhu Xun and Guinness World Records adjudicator Marco Frigatti are witnessing the attempt by a foreign challenger.

认证官马可·弗里加迪和主持人朱迅在现场认证一名外国挑战选手。 ←

前言

半个多世纪以来，《吉尼斯世界纪录大全》每年均跻身畅销书行列。1955年，第一本《吉尼斯世界纪录大全》出版，成为英国当年第一畅销书。迄今为止，其总销量已经超过1.15亿册，是最畅销的版权图书。

吉尼斯的故事

《吉尼斯世界纪录大全》已有55年的历史，它来源于一个人们在茶余饭后、学习工作期间反复讨论的问题。

1951年，在爱尔兰韦克斯福德郡（County Wexford）的一次狩猎聚会上，当时的英国吉尼斯啤酒公司执行董事休·比佛（Hugh Beaver）爵士提出疑问：欧洲飞得最快的鸟是什么？经过一番激烈争论，也翻遍了图书馆的资料，但他始终没有找到答案。

比佛爵士意识到，这些问题还没有人能回答，如果有一本书能为这类"争论"提供答案的话，公众将受益匪浅。当时，有一对孪生兄弟诺里斯·麦克沃特（Norris Mcwhiter）和罗斯·麦克沃特（Ross Mcwhiter）在伦敦开了一家实况调查公司，在他们的帮助下，比佛爵士迅速开始收集资料。1955年8月27日，第一本《吉尼斯世界纪录大全》装订成册，当年圣诞节前夕，该书即荣登

Presenter Wang Xuechun and Lin Hai were with the foreign record challengers in the studio of Zheng Da Zong Yi - Guinness World Records Special.

中央电视台主持人王雪纯、林海与外国选手在"正大综艺·吉尼斯中国之夜"节目现场。

英国畅销书榜首。

《吉尼斯世界纪录大全》现在被译成26种文字，在100多个国家发行，每年发行350多万册。通过国际公关活动，《吉尼斯世界纪录大全》每年都在不断拓展全球图书发行渠道。

《吉尼斯世界纪录大全》在中国

2000年，《吉尼斯世界纪录大全》第一部中文版在中国辽宁问世，此后连续几年推出中文版，在市场上获得了越来越多的关注。2006年，中国中央电视台与吉尼斯世界纪录有限公司联袂，录制和播出系列吉尼斯世界纪录的电视节目——《正大综艺·吉尼斯中国之夜》。通过国际化的运作手法，央视名主持的倾情演绎，给海内外观众带来了令人激动不已的体验。

吉尼斯世界纪录有限公司打破全球纪录汇集一册图书的惯例，欣然授权给中国国际出版集团旗下的海豚出版社，运作一部单纯荟萃中国人及中国人创造的文明的吉尼斯世界纪录的图书，借以展示中国迅速成长的侧影，让更多的海外人士，尤其是西方发达国家的普通人，从中国人挑战吉尼斯世界纪录的角度审视中国及中国人民，增进对中国以及中国人民的了解。

本书内容丰富，图文并茂地展示了中国及中国人创造的精彩：最大的宫殿、海拔最高的铁路线、年龄最大的歌剧演员，当然，也包括了中国古代人民创造的文明，如最早的书面文字、最早的地震仪、最长的古城墙……各个侧面的纪录，就像一面三棱镜，五彩缤纷地展示了中国的文明、发展与进步。吉尼斯纪录在中国越来越受到欢迎。

现在，欢迎你来到吉尼斯世界纪录中的中国的奇妙世界！你一定会赞叹那些值得在历史上留下名字的人们及不知名但却给我们留下宝贵财富的中国古代劳动人民。要申请纪录，还请登录吉尼斯世界纪录的网站办理。(www.guinnessworldrecords.com)

Guinness World Records adjudicator Marco Frigatti is presenting the certificate to the Chinese record holder Chen Yun.

认证官马可·弗里加迪为创造纪录成功的中国选手陈云颁发证书。↓

Natural World
自然世界

自然世界
Natural World

Largest doline
最大的岩溶漏斗

Xiao Zhai Tian Keng (The Great Doline) is the largest doline in the world. Situated in Sichuan Province of central southern China, this huge depression measures 500 m (1,600 ft) across and 660 m (2,165 ft) deep. Dolines are formed when limestone caves subside.

　　小寨天坑，位于中国中南部的四川地区，直径 500 米，深 660 米，是世界上最大的岩溶漏斗。↓

Deepest valley
最深的峡谷

The Yarlung Zangbo Valley in Tibet of China has an average depth of 5,000 m (16,400 ft), but explorers in 1994 discovered that its deepest point was 5,382 m (17,657 ft). The peaks of Namche Barwa (7,753 m, 25,436 ft) and Jala Peri (7,282 m, 23,891 ft) are just 21 km (13 miles) apart with the Yarlung Zangbo River between them, at an elevation of 2,440 m (8,000 ft).

　　雅鲁藏布江大峡谷，位于中国西藏，平均深度 5,000 米，是世界上最深的峡谷。有探险者在 1994 年发现其最深点为 5,382 米。

Highest river
海拔最高的河流

Of the major rivers of the world the highest one is the Yarlung Zangbo, which rises in Tibet of China, and runs for around 2,000 km (1,242 miles) in China, with an average elevation of around 4 km (2.4 miles), before entering India, where it is known as the Brahmaputra River. It enters the ocean at the Bay of Bengal, where it forms the world's largest delta.

　　雅鲁藏布江，发源于中国西藏，平均海拔 4,000 米，是世界上海拔最高的河流。在中国大地上绵延 2,000 千米，然后流入印度，在孟加拉湾入海，在那里形成世界上最大的三角洲。

Largest river to dry up
最大的断流河

The Yellow River (Huang He) is China's second longest river and is one of the greatest rivers of the world. For several months a year the 5,460 km (3,390 mile) river now dries up in Henan Province some 400 km (250 miles) before it reaches the sea.

　　黄河，是中国的第二大河，也是世界上最长的河流之一，长 5,460 千米，是世界上最长的断流河。现在这条河在入海前约 400 千米处的中国河南省境内，每年都会发生几个月的断流期。↑

Loudest singing sands
最响的沙漠

The world's loudest singing sands are at Mingshashan Mountain in western China. Recalling the noise made by a drum or a low-flying jet, their sounds are audible from as far away as 10 km (32,808 ft), can be as loud as 105 decibels, and exhibit a frequency of 95-105 hertz. The mechanism responsible for their sounds, however, remains controversial, but is believed to rely upon the sands' degree of wetness, as dry sands do not sing.

　鸣沙山，位于中国西部，它的声音在 10 千米以外都能听见，高达 105 分贝，频率为 95 ～ 105 赫兹。↓

Longest river with its entire drainage system in one country
流域在一国的最长河流

The longest river that has its entire drainage system within one country is the Yangtze River of China which measures 6,397 km (3,975 miles) long - the third longest river in the world, and the longest in Asia. The Yangtze River, as it is also known, has its headwaters in the glaciers of the Qinghai-Tibetan Plateau, heads eastwards across China and empties into the East China Sea.

　中国长江，发源于青藏高原，全长 6,397 千米，是世界第三长河，亚洲第一长河，也是流域在一国的最长河流。↑

Highest living fish
最高处生存的鱼

The highest living fish is the Tibetan loach (family Cobitidae), found at an altitude of 5,200 m (17,060 ft) in the Himalayas.

　　西藏条鳅，是在最高处生存的鱼，被发现于海拔5,200米的喜马拉雅山脉中。

Highest living mammal
生活在海拔最高处的哺乳动物

The highest-living mammal in the world is the large-eared pika (Ochtona macrotis), which has been recorded at a height of 6,130 m (20,112 ft) in high-altitude mountain ranges in Asia. The yak (Bos mutus) of Tibet and the Sichuanese Alps, China, climbs to an altitude of 6,100 m (20,013 ft) when foraging.

　　大耳鼠兔，是世界上生活在海拔最高处的哺乳动物。据记载，它生活在高达6,130米的亚洲山脉中，中国西藏和四川的野生牦牛只能爬到海拔6,100米处觅食。

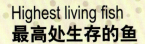

Highest and lowest desert
海拔最高和最低的沙漠

The People's Republic of China contains both the highest desert - the Qaidam Depression, which is 2,600 m (8,530 ft) above sea level, and the lowest desert, the Turpan Depression, which is 150 m (492 ft) below sea level.

　　海拔最高的沙漠，是中国的柴达木坳陷，海拔2,600米；海拔最低的沙漠，是中国的吐鲁番坳陷，低于海拔150米。

Heaviest panda cub born in captivity
出生时最重的饲养熊猫

The heaviest panda cub born in captivity weighed 218 g (7.6 oz) when he was born at the Wolong Giant Panda Research Centre, Chengdu, Sichuan Province, China on 7th August 2006. The cub is the first offspring of panda Zhang Ka, who was in labour for 34 hours itself, the longest recorded labour for a captive panda.

　　2006年8月7日，在中国四川省成都卧龙中国大熊猫保护研究中心，出生了一只最重的饲养熊猫，重达218克。它是熊猫"张卡"的第一个孩子。

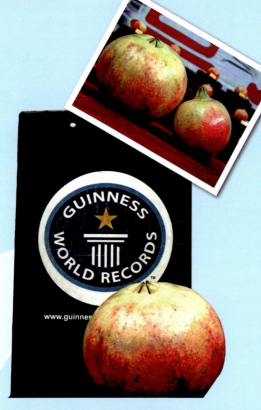

Heaviest pomegranate
最重的石榴

The heaviest pomegranate is 1.85 kg (4.08 lb) in weight and 48.7 cm (19.17 in) in circumference. It was grown in Aiguo village, Huili County, Sichuan Province, China, and was verified at the Pomegranate Competition organized by the People's Government of Huili County on 4th September 2009.

最重的石榴，重 1.85 千克，环围周长 48.7 厘米，产于中国四川省会理县爱国乡，是 2009 年 9 月 4 日，在会理县人民政府组织的"中国会理国际石榴节"上被测量的。←

Longest gourd
最长的丝瓜

The longest gourd measured 4.55 m (14 ft 11 in) when it was measured at the Beidaihe Jifa Agriculture Sightseeing Garden in Qinhuangdao, China, on 10th October 2008.

最长的丝瓜，长 4.55 米，是 2008 年 10 月 10 日，在中国秦皇岛北戴河集发农业观光园测出的。→

Highest islands
海拔最高的岛

Lake Orba, in Tibet, China, stands at 5,209 m (17,090 ft) above sea level. It contains several small islands.

海拔最高的岛，位于中国西藏的奥巴湖中，海拔 5,209 米。

Earliest prehistoric salamanders
最早的史前火蜥蜴

The earliest prehistoric salamanders date back 165 million years. Fossilised remains of thousands of individuals have been discovered in volcanic ash beds in China and Mongolia.

最早的史前火蜥蜴，大约生活在 1.65 亿年前，数千个个体的化石在中国和蒙古国的火山沉积层中被发现。

Heaviest taro
最重的芋头

The heaviest taro weighs 3.19 kg (7.03 lb) and was grown in Mingyang village, Fuding City, Fujian Province, China. The weight was verified at the taro competition organized by the people's Government of Fuding City at Taimu Mountain Scenic Spot, on 13th October 2009.

最重的芋头，重 3.19 千克，产于中国福建省福鼎茗洋村，于 2009 年 10 月 13 日被认证。→

Highest tree
海拔最高处生长的树

The highest altitude at which trees have been discovered is 4,600 m (15,092 ft), at which height a silver fir Abies squamata was found in southwestern China. Himalayan birch trees *Betula utilis* have also been discovered at this altitude. Specimens of *A. spectabilis*, a species closely related to *A.squamata*, have been found at an altitude of 4,267 m (14,000 ft) in the Himalayas.

　　鳞皮冷杉，被发现生长于海拔 4,600 米处，是迄今为止生长于海拔最高处的树木，被发现于中国的西南部。

Longest fossil-silicified tree trunk
最长的硅化木化石

The longest fossil silicified tree trunk measures 38 m (124 ft 8 in) and 1.2 m (3 ft 11 in) in basal diameter and consists of 33 sections, with roots, trunk and cross-section growth rings clearly preserved. The trunk, which was unearthed in Qitai County, Xinjiang, China, is displayed in the Shandong Tianyu Museum of Natural History, Shandong, China.

　　最长的硅化木化石，长 38 米，根部直径 1.2 米，产自中国新疆奇台县。现存放于中国山东省天宇自然博物馆。↓

Largest amphibian (present day)
现存最大的两栖动物

The largest amphibian is the giant salamander (*family Cryptobranchidae*), of which there are three species. The record-holder is the Chinese giant salamander (*Andrias davidianus*), which lives in mountain streams in northeastern, central and southern China. One record-breaking specimen collected in Hunan Province measured 1.8 m (5 ft 11 in) in length and weighed 65 kg (143 lb).

　　中国大鲵，是现存最大的两栖动物（俗名：娃娃鱼）。打破纪录的大鲵是在中国湖南省发现的，长 1.8 米，重 65 千克。→

Longest labour of a panda in captivity
饲养熊猫最长的分娩时间

The longest recorded labour for a captive panda is 34 hours and belongs to panda Zhang Ka, as she gave birth to her first cub - and the largest panda cub born in captivity weighing 218 g (7.6 oz) - at the Wolong Giant Panda Research Centre, Chengdu, Sichuan Province, China, on 7th August 2006.

饲养熊猫最长的分娩时间,是 34 小时。由大熊猫"张卡"于 2006 年 8 月 7 日,在中国成都卧龙自然保护区大熊猫研究中心创造。

Longest feathers on a wild bird
野生鸟类身上最长的羽毛

The longest feathers recorded from any species of wild bird are the central tail feathers of Reeves' pheasant (*Syrmaticus reevesii*), native to the mountains of central and northern China. These feathers sometimes exceed 2.4 m (8 ft) in length, and if thrown up in flight they act as a brake, helping the bird to drop vertically down into the cover of trees to escape any would-be attacker.

野生鸟类身上最长的羽毛,是白冠长尾雉身上的中央尾羽,这些羽毛有的长达 2.4 米以上。此种鸟原产于中国中部和北部山区。

Largest amethyst geode
最大的紫水晶洞

The largest amethyst geode measures 3 m (9 ft 10 in) long, 1.8 m (5 ft 10 in) wide, 2.2 m (7 ft 2 in) high and weighs 13 tonnes (28,660 lb). It is displayed in Shandong Tianyu Museum of Natural History (China) in Shandong, China.

最大的紫水晶洞,长 3 米,高 2.2 米,宽 1.8 米,重达 13 吨。目前存放于中国山东省天宇自然博物馆。↓

Largest agate
最大的玛瑙

The largest agate measures 61,090.2 kg (134,680.84 lb) and was verified at an event organized by the Development & Reform Commission of Fuxin Municipal Government in Fuxin City, Liaoning Province, China, on 25th October 2009.

最大的玛瑙,重61,090.2千克,于2009年10月25日,在中国阜新由阜新市发展与改革委员会组织的一个活动中被认证。↓

玛瑙王等四项吉尼斯世界纪录认证

中国·阜新

Largest dinosaur fossil site
最大的恐龙化石群

Based upon the number of finds since their discovery in 2008 in Zhucheng City, China's Shandong fossil bone beds comprise the world's biggest dinosaur fossil site. According to Zhao Zijin of Beijing's Institute of Vertebrate Palaeontology and Palaeoanthropology, this site has already yielded more than 7,600 fossils, dating from the Late Cretaceous Period (100 million to 65 million years ago). Among the most notable finds so far is a 2 m (6 ft 6.74 in) long skull of a ceratopsian dinosaur, the first Late Cretaceous example from this group of horned dinosaurs ever recorded outside North America, and which included such famous dinosaurs as Triceratops and Styracosaurus.

中国山东省诸城恐龙化石群，被证明是目前世界上已发现的规模最大、化石储量最丰富的恐龙化石群。

Longest giant panda pregnancy
最长的大熊猫孕期

The longest recorded pregnancy for a giant panda (*Ailuropoda melanoleuca*) lasted 200 days by panda Shu Lan, who gave birth to a healthy male cub on 21st October 2004 at Chengdu Research Base for Giant Pandas, Sichuan Province, China. The average pregnancy for a giant panda is 95-160 days.

最长的大熊猫孕期，是 200 天。由熊猫〝蜀兰〞于 2004 年 10 月 21 日，在中国成都大熊猫繁育研究基地创造。它产下了一只健康的雄性小熊猫，而一般熊猫的平均孕期为 95 ～ 160 天。

Largest turquoise
最大的绿松石

The largest turquoise measures 1.03 m (3 ft 5 in) long, 1.06 m (3 ft 6 in) high, 26 cm (10 in) thick and weighs 225 kg (496 lb). It is housed in the Shandong Tianyu Museum of Natural History, Shandong Province, China.

最大的绿松石，长 1.03 米，高 1.06 米，厚 0.26 米，重 225 千克，现存放于中国山东省天宇自然博物馆。

Largest Sinosauropteryx fossil
最大的中华龙鸟化石

The largest Sinosauropteryx fossil measures 3.8 m (12 ft 5 in) long. It is housed in the Shandong Tianyu Museum of Natural History in Shandong Province, China.

最大的中华龙鸟化石，长 3.8 米，现存放于中国山东省天宇自然博物馆。

Largest scheelite crystal
最大的白钨矿晶体

The largest scheelite crystal measures 0.4 m (1 ft 3.7 in) long, 0.3 m (11.8 in) tall and 0.15m (5.9 in) thick. It is kept at the Shandong Tianyu Museum of Natural History in Shandong Province, China.

最大的白钨矿晶体，长 0.4 米，高 0.3 米，宽 0.15 米，现存放于中国山东省天宇自然博物馆。↑

Largest ruby
最大的红宝石

The largest ruby weighs 8,184 g (288 oz) and measures 130 x 138 x 145 mm (5.118 x 5.433 x 5.708 in). It is owned by Beijing Fugui Tianshi Jewellery Co., Ltd. of Beijing, China.

最大的红宝石，体积为 130 毫米 ×138 毫米 × 145 毫米，重 8,184 克，现存放于中国北京。↓

Most complete feathered dinosaur fossil
最完整的长羽毛的恐龙化石

In April 2001 a complete fossil of Sinornithosaurus millenii, a relative of the Velociraptor, was discovered by farmers at the Yixian Formation Fossil Bed, Liaoning Province, China. It is completely covered in downy fluff and primitive feathers and was found between two slabs of fine grained rock estimated to be 130 million years old. It resembles a large duck with a long tail and is approximately 60 cm (2 ft) long.

　　最完整的长羽毛的恐龙化石，于 2001 年 4 月，在中国辽宁省义县组地层被发现。该化石长约 60 厘米，像一只长着大尾巴的大鸭子，它夹在两块约有 1.3 亿年历史的幼粒岩石之间，完全被绒毛覆盖。

Most plant species grafted on to the same plant
单株嫁接品种最多的植物

The record number of different plant species grafted on to the same plant is 513 varieties of chrysanthemum on to the host chrysanthemum plant. It was created for the 9th China (Xiaolan, Zhongshan) Chrysanthemum Exhibition in Xiaolan Town, China, on 23rd November 2007.

　　单株嫁接品种最多的植物，是 2007 年 11 月 23 日，在第九届中国（中山小榄）菊花展览会上展出的单株嫁接 513 个品种的大丽菊。↓

Most restricted distribution of any bear
熊家族最有限的分布区域

The giant panda (*Ailuropoda melanoleuca*) has the most restricted distribution for any bear, being limited to six small mountainous areas in Sichuan, Shaanxi and Gansu Provinces along the eastern rim of the Tibetan Plateau in southwestern China, yielding a total range of only 5,900 km² (2,277 miles²).

　　大熊猫中的熊家族最有限的分布区域，位于中国西南部，西藏高原东部沿线的四川、陕西、甘肃等省的六个小的高山地区，面积总计 5,900 平方千米。

Most southerly ice in the northern hemisphere
北半球最南边的结冰处

The most southerly place in the northern hemisphere, where the seas are normally closed by ice for part of every year, is in the Bohai Sea, off the coast of China at about Lat. 37°48´ N, which is further south than Athens, Greece.

北半球最南边的结冰处，位于中国的渤海，北纬 37 度 48 分，比希腊的雅典还要更靠南。

Oldest ceratopsian dinosaur
最老的角龙类恐龙

The oldest ceratopsian dinosaur discovered to date is Liaoceratops. It was discovered by Xing Xu (China) of the Chinese Academy of Sciences, Beijing, in the Yixian Formation, a fossil-rich rock bed in northeast China. The rocks in which the skulls and skeletons were found date the creature at having lived 120-145 million years ago. This herbivore was a precurser to the more well known Triceratops. The discovery was announced on 21st March 2002 in the journal *Nature*.

辽宁角龙，是目前发现的最古老的角龙类恐龙，由中国科学院的徐星在中国辽宁省义县组化石床发现。

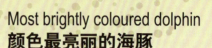

Most brightly coloured dolphin
颜色最亮丽的海豚

The world's most brightly coloured dolphin is the Chinese pink dolphin (*Sousa chinensis chinensis*), which is a subspecies of the Indo-Pacific hump-backed dolphin. A popular if nowadays increasingly endangered tourist attraction in Hong Kong harbour, the adult of this dolphin, which measures 2.2 m - 2.5 m (7 ft - 8 ft) long and weighs 150 kg - 250 kg (330 lb - 550 lb), is noted for its bright pink-coloured skin. Its eyecatching colour is not due to skin pigmentation, however, but instead it results from the presence just beneath the surface of numerous blood vessels that are used for thermoregulatory purposes. They help to prevent the dolphin from overheating during exertion by dilating, releasing heat that has built up inside the dolphin's body. When newly born, however, the Chinese pink dolphin is actually black, changing to grey as a youngster, and ultimately to pink as it matures. Also pink in colour, but rather less bright, is the skin of the Amazonian river dolphin or boto (*Inia geoffrensis*).

颜色最亮丽的海豚，是中国的粉海豚，它是印度洋——太平洋驼背海豚的一个亚种。在中国香港海湾有一只成年海豚，长约 2.2～2.5 米，重 150～250 千克，以其亮粉色的皮肤闻名，吸引了很多游客。

Oldest elephant
最老的大象

The oldest elephant ever was Lin Wang, an Asian elephant (*Elephas maximus*), who died on 26th February 2003 aged 86, at Taipei Zoo, Taiwan, China.

最老的大象，是亚洲象"林旺"，2003年2月26日，在台湾的台北动物园去世，时年 86 岁。↓

Oldest cultivated plant for products
最古老的耕作物

Among the world's oldest cultivated plants that are used primarily for products such as clothing and medicine is the hemp plant (*Cannabis sativa*). It was first cultivated in China 5,000 years ago; indeed the earliest documented example is a 6,000-year-old piece of cloth, made from hemp fibre and discovered amongst ancient human habitat sites in Asia.

最古老的耕作物，是麻，最早于5,000 年前在中国种植。目前最早的实证，是一块有 6,000 年历史的由麻织成的布片，它是在亚洲古人类居住地被发现的。

Oldest marsupial, prehistoric
最古老的史前有袋动物

The oldest known relative of all marsupials is Sinodelphys szalayi, a fossil of which was discovered in Liaoning Province, China, in 2001 and dated to 125 million years old. A Sino-American research team, including Ji Qiang and Zhe Xi Luo (both China), named the fossil and concluded it measured 15 cm (5.9 in) long and weighed 30 g (1.05 oz) approximately.

最古老的史前有袋动物，是中国袋兽。2001 年，中美研究团队在中国辽宁省发现其化石并为其命名。该化石体长 15 厘米，重约 30 克，有 1.25 亿年历史。

Oldest tyrannosauroid
最老的暴龙

Dilong paradoxus, the oldest known ancestor of Tyrannosaurus Rex, lived between 128 and 139 million years ago - some 60-70 million years before T-Rex. It measured some 1.5 m (5 ft) in length, stood on two legs, and had longer arms than T-Rex. There is also evidence that this creature had hair-like protofeathers on its jaw and the tip of its tail. Dilong paradoxus was discovered in the famous fossil beds of Liaoning Province, China, by a team of Chinese and American palaeontologists, and announced in the journal *Nature* in October 2004.

暴龙科的奇异帝龙,生活在 1.28 亿~ 1.39 亿年前, 比同科的霸王龙早 6000 万~ 7000 万年, 是霸王龙已知的最早的祖先。奇异帝龙的化石被发现于中国辽宁省, 该化石长 1.5 米, 两脚站立, 前臂比霸王龙长。

Oldest fossilised embryo
最古老的胚胎化石

The oldest fossilised embryos date back around 500 million years. Around 100 embryos, of Markuelia hunanensis, an extinct species of worm, were discovered in Hunan, southern China, by a team from Bristol University, Bristol, UK, and Peking University, Beijing, China. Their results were announced in the journal *Nature* in January 2004.

最古老的胚胎化石, 是被英国布里斯托尔大学和中国北京大学组成的团队在中国湖南省发现的, 约有 5 亿年历史。

Oldest flowering plant
最古老的开花植物化石

On 3rd May 2002, scientists announced the discovery of the fossilised remains of the earliest flowering plant discovered to date. At least 125 million years old, and named Archaefructus sinensis (ancient fruit from China), it was found in a slab of stone in northeast China and is possibly the ancestor of all the flowering plants in the world today. Its closest living relative may be the water lilly, as the ancient plant lived in clear shallow water with its flowers and seeds extending above the surface.

最古老的开花植物化石, 被命名为"中华古果"。此发现于 2002 年 5 月 3 日被科学家公布。据考证, 距今至少有 1.25 亿年历史。

Oldest panda in captivity
年纪最大的饲养熊猫

The oldest panda ever in captivity was panda Dudu, who was born in Chengdu by 1962 and lived for most of her life in Wuhan Zoo, Hubei, China, until her death on 22nd July 1999 aged 37.

年纪最大的饲养熊猫, 名叫"都都"。1962 年生于中国成都, 1999 年 7 月 22 日老死于武汉动物园, 时年 37 岁。

Smallest pterodactyl
最小的翼龙

The smallest known species of Pterodactyls is presently the forest pterosaur Nemicolopterus crypticus. Discovered in the Early Cretaceous Jiufotang Formation (dating to around 120 million years ago) in Yaolugou, Jianchang County, Huludao City, in China's northeastern Liaoning Province, its remains yield a near-complete skeleton of a sub-adult specimen. It revealed that this tiny species sported a wingspan of just under 25 cm (9.84 in), comparable to a sparrow's, and weighed a mere 30 - 50 g (1 - 1.7 oz).

最小的翼龙，是"隐居森林翼龙"，距今约1.2亿年。其化石发现于中国辽宁省葫芦岛建昌县，翼展仅25厘米，大致相当于一只麻雀大小，重约30～50克。

Smallest species of dinosaur
最小的恐龙

The smallest species of dinosaur is the feathered Microraptor zhaoianus, measuring a total length of 39 cm (15.3 in), of which 24 cm (9.4 in) is its tail. A fossil of the species was discovered in Chaoyang, Liaoning Province, China, in 1999, and dated back to 110-120 million years ago.

最小的恐龙，是有羽毛的赵氏小盗龙。长39厘米，其中尾巴长达24厘米，其化石于1999年在中国辽宁省被发现，距今约1.1亿～1.2亿年。

Tallest stalagmite
最高的石笋

The tallest stalagmite in the world measures 70 m (230 ft) in height. It is located in Zhi Jin Cave, Guizhou Province, China.

最高的石笋，位于中国贵州省织金洞内，高70米。

Tallest herba cistanches
最高的肉苁蓉

The world's tallest herba cistanches (*Cistanche deserticola*) measured 1.95 m (6 ft 4 in) on 15th August 2006. It was collected from the desert of Inner Mongolia, China, by Yongmao Chen and identified by the College of Life Sciences of the Inner Mongolia University, China. It was preserved by Yongmao Chen.

最高的肉苁蓉，长1.95米，采自中国内蒙古的沙漠，经过中国内蒙古大学生命科学学院鉴定，于2006年8月15日测量。现由陈永茂收藏。

Thickest point of the Earth's crust
最厚的地壳

The Himalaya mountains in China is where the Earth's crust is thickest, at around 75 km (46 miles).

最厚的地壳，位于中国的喜马拉雅山脉，约75千米。

Rarest marine mammal
最稀有的海生哺乳动物

The baiji, or Yangtze River Dolphin (*Lipotes vexillifer*), has an estimated population of only a few dozen in the whole world. The population is still falling owing to competition of fisheries, accidental capture in nets, pollution, disturbance and habitat destruction. The baiji is still killed for its meat and oil. The few survivors live mainly in the middle reaches of the Yangtze River, China. Despite being a national treasure in China, the baiji is expected to become extinct in the near future.

最稀有的海生哺乳动物，是中国的白鳍豚。目前全世界只有几十只白鳍豚，主要生活在中国长江的中游。

Science, Technology and Engineering

科技与工程

科技与工程
Science, Technology
and Engineering

Earliest bioluminescent pigs
第一头荧光猪

The world's first fully bioluminescent, transgenic pigs were born in 2005, created by a scientific team from National Taiwan University's Department of Animal Science and Technology. They added DNA from bioluminescent jellyfish to approximately 265 pig embryos, which were in turn implanted into eight different sows. Four of these sows duly became pregnant, and three male bioluminescent piglets were born. Even in daylight they have a greenish tinge, which becomes a torch-like glow if blue light is shone on them in the dark, and not only their skin but also their internal organs glow. Stem cells taken from them will be used to trace human diseases, as the green-glowing protein that the pigs produce can be readily observed without the need for biopsies or invasive tests.

　　第一头荧光猪，于 2005 年，由台湾大学动物科学技术学系科研团队研发。

Busiest railway network for freight (country)
拥有最繁忙的铁路货运交通网的国家

China's national railway network carried 2.178 billion tonnes of freight during 2004, making it the world's busiest for cargo. The USA was the second, with 1.673 billion tonnes, and Russia third, with 1.16 billion tonnes, according to the International Union of Railways (UIC).

　　拥有最繁忙的铁路货运交通网的国家，是中国。2004 年货运量达到 21.78 亿吨。

Highest revolving door
最高的旋转门

The tallest revolving door measures 4.8 m (15 ft 9 in) and is located in the Novotel Citygate Hong Kong Hotel in Tung Chung, Hong Kong, China. The door was measured during the Hotel's official opening on 12th June 2006.

　　最高的旋转门，位于中国香港东涌的诺富特东荟城酒店，高 4.8 米。于 2006 年 6 月 12 日，在该酒店正式营业时测量。

Busiest port for containers
最繁忙的集装箱港口

In 2004 the port of Hong Kong, China, handled 22 million standard shipping containers (TEUs), making it the world's busiest container port. The port has nine terminals occupying 285 ha (704 acres) with 24 deep-water berths between them.

最繁忙的集装箱港口，是中国香港港口。2004 年吞吐量达 2,200 万个标准集装箱。

Earliest mechanical clock
最早的机械钟

The earliest mechanical clock, i.e. one with an escapement, was completed in China in 725 AD by Yi Xing and Liang Lingzan.

最早的机械钟，于公元 725 年，由中国的一行和梁令瓒发明制造。

Earliest gun
最早的枪

Gunpowder may have been invented in China, India, Arabia or Europe in the 13th century. Although it cannot be accepted as proven, it is believed that the earliest guns were constructed both in China and in Northern Africa c. 1250. The invention of the gun certainly dates from before 1326 for which there is documentary evidence, and references thereafter become more frequent. The earliest known example of a gun was found in the ruins of the castle of Monte Varino in Italy. The castle was destroyed in 1341.

虽然未经完全证实，但人们相信，最早的枪，是存在于 1250 年左右，在中国和北非均有制造。

Earliest man-made bioluminescent fish
最早的人造荧光鱼

Created in 2001 by H.J. Tsai, a professor of fisheries science at National Taiwan University, subsequently sold by the Taipei-based Taikong Corporation, and dubbed Frankenfish, the world's first man-made bioluminescent fish are green-glowing specimens of the zebra fish, a popular aquarium species, whose bioluminescence is due to the introduction of jellyfish DNA. Officially known as night pearls or TK-1, they were followed in 2003 by a second artificial strain of bioluminescent zebra fish, the TK-2, this time glowing red rather than green, having received a gene for red bioluminescence from a species of red-glowing coral.

最早的人造荧光鱼，于 2001 年，由台湾大学鱼类科学教授蔡怀桢培育。

Earliest use of forensic entomology
法医昆虫学的最早应用

According to internationally renowned forensic biologist, Mark Benecke (Germany), the study of insects recovered from crime scenes and corpses can be traced back to a 13th century medico-legal text book entitled *Xi Yuan Lu* (The Washing Away of Wrongs) by Song Ci (China), a lawyer and death investigator. When called upon to investigate a fatal stabbing in a rice field, Song Ci asked workers to lay down their sickles; soon afterwards, blow flies were attracted to one particular sickle covered in invisible traces of blood, compelling its owner to confess to the crime. It is now known that certain blow flies such as Calliphora vomitoria have a preference for laying their eggs in fresh blood.

据国际知名的法医生物学家马克·贝内克（德国人）称，对犯罪现场和尸体上的昆虫进行研究，可追溯至13世纪的法医文献《洗冤录》。这是世界上最早的一部法医学名著，由中国宋代的宋慈所著。

Earliest use of rockets
火箭的第一次应用

Propelled by gunpowder, flying fireworks (charcoal-saltpetre-sulfur) were described by Zeng Gongliang of China in 1042. War rockets originated in 1245 near Hangzhou, China (the capital of China between 1127 and 1278). However, the first use of true rockets was reported in 1232 during the battle of Kaifeng.

火箭的第一次应用，是在1232年的中国开封府战役中。

Earliest use of a crossbow
最早使用的弩

The earliest reliable record of the use of a crossbow was in 341 BC at the Battle of Maling, Linyi, China.

最早使用弩的可靠记录，是在公元前341年中国的马陵之战中。

First restaurant with robot waiting staff
最早使用机器人服务的餐厅

Robot Kitchen in Hong Kong, China, opened in July 2006. It has two robot staff members capable of taking orders from customers and delivering their meals to them. A third robot is being constructed that should be able to perform simple culinary tasks, such as preparing omelettes and flipping burgers.

最早使用机器人服务的餐厅，是中国香港的机器人餐厅。于2006年7月营业，这里有两名机器人服务员为顾客点菜和送菜，还有一个机器人可以做一些简单的烹饪工作，如煎蛋或烙饼。

Earliest seismograph
最早的地震仪

The first modern seismographs were developed in 1848, but the earliest form of earthquake-detecting equipment can be traced all the way back to 132 AD and the Han Dynasty (202 BC - 220 AD) in China. The first device was designed by the then Chinese Royal Astronomer, Zhang Heng, who built a 15 cm (6 in) bronze vessel containing a pendulum. Any minor movement in the ground would cause the pendulum to dislodge balls which would fall into the mouths of bronze toads, signalling an earthquake.

第一个具有现代意义的地震仪，发明于 1848 年，但最早形式探测地震的仪器，可追溯至公元 132 年，由中国汉代天文学家张衡设计。↓

Fastest lift (elevator)
最快的电梯

Two high-speed lifts installed by Toshiba Elevator and Building Systems (Japan) in Taipei 101, situated in Taipei, Taiwan, China, have a maximum speed of 1,010 m/min (3,313 ft/min), equivalent to 60.6 km/h (37.6 mph). The lifts take just 40 seconds from ground level to the 89th floor, situated at 382 m (1,253 ft), and have atmospheric pressure regulatory systems to avoid discomfort (ears "popping") for the occupants.

最快的电梯，是东芝电梯建筑系统集团公司安装在台湾台北的 101 大楼中的两部电梯。其运行速度高达 1,010 米／分钟，相当于 60.6 千米／小时,仅需 40 秒就可从地面抵达 89 层 (382 米)。

Fastest maximum operating speed for a train
运行时速最快的火车

On the 114 km (70.84 miles) long Beijing-Tianjin Intercity Railway line in China, trains run at a maximum operating speed (MOS) of 350 km/h (217.48 mph). Tests have shown an unmodified capability of 394 km/h (244.82 mph) but the speed has been limited for safety reasons.

　　运行时速最快的火车，是中国的京津城际列车（北京—天津）。运行在全长 114 千米的铁路线上，最高时速为 350 千米／小时。↓

Fastest train in regular public service
最快的公共交通列车

The magnetically levitated (maglev) train linking China's Shanghai International Airport and the city's financial district, reaches a top speed of 431 km/h (267.8 mph) on each 30 km (18 miles) run. The train, built by Germany's Transrapid International, had its official maiden run on 31st December 2002.

　　最快的公共交通列车，是中国上海的磁悬浮列车。它连接了该城市的金融区和浦东国际机场，单程 30 千米，最高时速达 431 千米／小时。2002 年 12 月 31 日首次投入运营。

Heaviest building moved intact
最重的楼房完整平移

The heaviest building moved intact is the Fu Gang Building at West Bank Road, Wuzhou, Guangxi Province of China. It was successfully relocated by the Guangzhou Luban Corporation on 10th November 2004.The building weighs 15,140.4 metric tonnes (33.3 million lb) and is 34 m (111 ft) tall. The building was moved 35.62 m (116 ft 10.3 in) horizontally and it took 11 days to complete the relocation.

中国广西省梧州西堤路福港楼，是实现完整平移的最重建筑物，总重量 15,140.4 吨，高 34 米，历时 11 天，平移了 35.62 米。↑

Highest observation deck
最高的观景台

The highest observation deck is located on the 100th floor, 477.96 m (1568 ft 1 in), of the Shanghai World Financial Center in Pudong, China.

　　最高的观景台，位于中国上海浦东的上海环球金融中心的第 100 层上，距地面 477.96 米。

Highest commercial bungee jump
最高的商业蹦极跳

The highest commercial bungee jump facility is 233 m (764 ft 5 in) high and is located on the Macao Tower in Macao, China. The facility was inaugurated with a jump by film star Edison Chen (China) on 17th December 2006.

最高的商业蹦极跳，设在 233 米高的中国澳门的澳门塔。2006 年 12 月 17 日，影星陈冠希在此进行首跳。

Highest altitude reached by a hovercraft
气垫船到达的最高海拔

The highest altitude reached by a hovercraft is 4,983 m (16,348 ft), achieved by Neste Enterprise and her crew of ten at the navigable source of China's Yangtze River on 11th June 1990. Operating hovercraft at such altitudes is problematic both because of the challenging terrain and the thin air, which makes hovering more difficult.

1990 年 6 月 11 日，载有 10 名工作人员的 Neste Enterprise 气垫船开到了中国长江上游的适航段，该适航段海拔 4,983 米。此为气垫船到达的最高海拔位置。

Heaviest weight lifted by a crane
起重机吊起的最重货物

The heaviest weight lifted by a crane is 20,133 tonnes (44,385,667.25 lb), achieved by the "Taishan" crane at Yantai Raffles Shipyard, Yantai, China, on 18th April 2008.

2008 年 4 月 18 日，"泰山"起重机在中国烟台莱佛士造船厂吊起 20,133 吨满载驳船。这是目前为止起重机吊起的最重货物。↓

Highest railway line
海拔最高的铁路线

The Qinghai-Tibet Railway in China, completed in October 2005, is the world's highest railway. Most of the 1,956 km (1,215 miles) long line lies at 4,000 m (13,123 ft) above sea level, with the highest point reaching an altitude of 5,072 m (16,640 ft). Service was open to the public in 2006. Passenger carriages will be pressurised similar to aircraft cabins and oxygen masks are available.

　　海拔最高的铁路线，是 2005 年 10 月修建完工的中国青藏铁路，全长 1,956 千米。其中大部分路段海拔 4,000 米，最高处可达 5,072 米。青藏铁路于 2006 年全线通车。↑

Highest trail
海拔最高的公路

The highest trail in the world is a 13 km (8 miles) stretch of the Gandise, between Khaleb and Xinjifu, Tibet, China, which in two places exceeds 6,080 m (19,948 ft).

　　海拔最高的公路，位于冈底斯山上，长 13 千米，在中国西藏卡勒布和辛齐夫之间，两地海拔均在 6,080 米以上。

Highest Airport
海拔最高的机场

Bamda Airport in eastern Tibet, China, lies at 4,739 m (15,548 ft) above sea level.

　　海拔最高的机场，是中国西藏的邦达机场，海拔 4,739 米。

Largest hydroelectric project
最大的水电站工程

The Three Gorges Dam in China is a massive project that will generate power for China's expanding economy, as well as control flooding in the Yangtze River. In May 2006 the huge dam wall, measuring 2,309 m (7,575 ft) long by 185 m (607 ft) high was completed. The dam was fully operational in 2009 upon the final installation of its generators.

最大的水电站工程，是中国的三峡大坝。2006 年 5 月竣工，全长 2,309 米，高 185 米。于 2009 年安装最后的发电机后投入使用。

Largest wood fired ceramic kiln
最大的柴烧瓷窑

The largest wood fired ceramic kiln is the Jingdezhen Zhen Kiln measuring 260.03 cubic meters (9,183 cubic feet). It was certified at the Exhibition Region of Old Kiln Folk Customs in Jingdezhen City, Jiangxi Province, China, on 22nd October 2009.

　　最大的柴烧瓷窑，是中国景德镇的镇窑，容积为 260.03 立方米。于 2009 年 10 月 22 日，在中国景德镇古窑民俗博览区被认证。↑

Largest palace
最大的宫殿

The Imperial Palace in the centre of Beijing, China, covers a rectangle measuring 960 x 750 m (3,150 x 2,460 ft) over an area of 72 ha (178 acres). The outline survives from the construction of the third Ming Emperor, Yongle (1403-1424), but owing to constant reconstruction work, most of the intra-mural buildings (five halls and 17 palaces) are from the 18th century.

The Palace of Versailles, 23 km (14 miles) south-west of Paris, France, is 580 m (1,902 ft) long and has a facade with 375 windows. The building, completed in 1682 for Louis XIV, occupied over 30,000 workmen under Jules Hardouin-Mansart (1646-708).

最大的宫殿，是中国北京的故宫，呈 960 米 × 750 米的长方形，占地面积超过 72 公顷。↓

Highest altitude railway tunnel
海拔最高的铁路隧道

The Fenghuo Mount Railway Tunnel is situated at 4,905 m (16,092 ft) on the Qinghai-Tibet Railway as it passes over the Qinghai-Tibet Plateau in China. It is 1,338 m (4,390 ft) long and was constructed between 18th October 2001 and 30th September 2003.

海拔最高的铁路隧道，是中国的青藏铁路穿越青藏高原时经过的风火山铁路隧道，海拔 4,905 米，全长 1,338 米。于 2001 年 10 月 18 日至 2003 年 9 月 30 日间开凿。

Highest building to house a hotel
位置最高的酒店

The Park Hyatt Shanghai in Pudong, China, is the highest hotel in the world. It occupies 79 to 93 floors of the Shanghai World Financial Center.

位置最高的酒店，是中国上海浦东的柏悦酒店。位于中国上海环球金融中心的 79 ~ 93 层。↓

Highest library
位置最高的
图书馆

The library on the 60th floor of the JW Marriott Hotel at Tomorrow Square in Shanghai, China, is situated at 230.9 m (757 ft 6 in) above street level. Membership is available to the public and the 103 shelves in the library contains an ever-expanding collection of Chinese and English books.

位置最高的图书馆，位于中国上海明天广场万豪酒店 60 楼，距地面 230.9 米。

Largest advertisement on a building
最大的楼体广告

The largest advertisement on a building was for the *Financial Times* newspaper covering an area of 19,125.48 m² (205,865.02 ft²). It was on display on the north and east side of the International Finance Centre in Hong Kong, China, from 22nd October to 10th November 2003.

最大的楼体广告，是 2003 年 10 月 22 日至 11 月 10 日期间，在中国香港国际金融中心二期大楼北面和东面楼体上展出的巨幅《金融时报》广告，覆盖面积达 19,125.48 平方米。

Largest rotating three-sided billboard (advertisement)
最大的三面翻广告牌

The rotating three-sided advertisement board attached to the walls of the Jianianhua Mansion of the Chongqing Financial Real Estate Company in Chongqing, China, has a total surface area of 5,748 m² (61,871 ft²). It was opened on 5th February 2005 and covers all four sides of the building.

最大的三面翻广告牌，置于中国重庆金融街房地产公司的嘉年华大厦外墙上，覆盖了建筑的四面墙面，总面积达 5,748 平方米，于 2005 年 2 月 5 日投入使用。

Longest ancient city wall
最长的古城墙

The ancient city wall of Nanjing in China's Jiangsu Province was 33.6 km (21 miles) when first constructed in the Ming Dynasty (1368 - 1644), and around two thirds of it remains. It has an average height of around 12 m (40 ft) and contains 13 gates.

最长的古城墙，是位于中国江苏省南京的明城墙，总长 33.6 千米。始建于明代（1368 ～ 1644 年），现存三分之二，平均高度约 12 米，有 13 座城门。

Longest rubber dam
最长的橡胶坝

The longest rubber dam measures 1,135 m (3,723 ft) long and consists of 16 sections, each section being 70 m (229 ft) long. The Xiaobudong Rubber Dam is situated on the Yihe River, Shandong Province, China, and was completed 1st July 1997.

最长的橡胶坝，是小埠东橡胶坝。位于中国山东省，全长 1,135 米，由 16 段组成，每段 70 米，于 1997 年 7 月 1 日建成。

Largest illuminated advertising sign
最大的灯光广告标志

The largest illuminated advertising sign measured 91.5 m (298 ft 6 in) wide by 55 m (180 ft 5 in) high and covered an area of 5,033 m² (54,174 ft²) on the external wall of Tai Sing Container and Godown Centre, Qing Yi Island, New Territories, Hong Kong, China. Depicting a dragon, it was constructed on 18th December 1999 and contained over 800,000 light bulbs.

最大的灯光广告标志，是一个龙的形象，宽 91.5 米，高 55 米，外墙覆盖面积 5,033 平方米，位于中国香港新界青衣岛的大生货柜仓库中心，使用了 80 万个灯泡。

Largest airport passenger terminal building
最大的机场客运航站楼

The Hong Kong International Airport passenger terminal building is 1.3 km (0.8 mile) long and covers 550,000 m² (5,920,150 ft²). The building's design incorporates a Y-shaped concourse and is the world's largest single airport building. Just the baggage hall of this gargantuan building is as big as the Yankee Stadium in New York (it could hold five Boeing 747s parked wing tip to wing tip). Served by 48 aircraft parking stands with boarding gates and air bridges, the terminal has a design capacity of 45 million passengers a year, arriving on 460 flights every day. There are 3 km (1.8 miles) of moving walkways, 55,000 m² (592,015 ft²) of glass cladding and around 117,000 m² (1,259,400 ft²) of carpeting.

最大的机场客运航站楼，是中国香港国际机场客运航站楼，全长 1.3 千米，占地 55 万平方米，设计呈 "Y" 字型，是目前世界上最大的独立机场建筑物。

Largest square
最大的广场

Tian'anmen (Gate of Heavenly Peace) Square in Beijing, described as the navel of China, is the world's largest square. It covers 39.6 ha (98 acres).

最大的广场，是中国北京的天安门广场，占地面积 39.6 公顷。↓

Longest bridge, steel arch bridge
最长的 钢结构拱桥

The world's longest steel arch bridge is the Lupu Bridge, Shanghai, China. It has a span of 550 m (1,804 ft) over the Huangpu River. It was constructed over three years and opened on 28th June 2003.

最长的钢结构拱桥, 是中国上海卢浦大桥。主跨 550 米长, 横跨黄浦江。历时三年建造, 于 2003 年 6 月 28 日投入使用。↓

Longest covered promenade
最长的有顶长廊

The Long Corridor in the Summer Palace in Beijing, China, runs for 728 m (2,388 ft) and is built entirely of wood and divided by crossbeams into 273 sections.

最长的有顶长廊, 是颐和园长廊。位于中国北京的颐和园内, 全长 728 米, 木结构, 由大梁分隔成 273 间。→

Longest escalators
最长的电动扶梯

The world's longest escalator system is Hong Kong's Central Hillside Escalator Link. The 800 m (2,624 ft) long system of covered moving walkways carries commuters between the Mid-levels district and Central Market close to the waterfront on Hong Kong Island.

最长的电动扶梯, 是中国香港的山坡自动扶梯, 长 800 米, 连接中环商业区及半山住宅区。

Longest wall
最长的墙

The Great Wall of China is the longest wall in the world and has a main-line length of 3,460 km (2,150 miles), plus 3,530 km (2,195 miles) of branches and spurs. Its height varies from 4.5 to 12 m (15 to 39 ft) and it is up to 9.8 m (32 ft) thick. It runs from Shanhaiguan, on the Gulf of Bohai, to Yumenguan and Yangguan and was kept in repair up to the 16th century. Some 51.5 km (32 miles) of the wall have been destroyed since 1966, and part of the wall was blown up to make way for a dam in July 1979.

最长的墙，是中国的长城。主体部分有 3,460 千米，还有 3,530 千米的分支，高度从 4.5 米到 12 米不等，最厚处达到 9.8 米。自公元前 221 年开始修建，一直延续到 16 世纪，东起渤海湾的山海关，西至玉门关和阳关。

Largest single tomb
最大的独立陵墓

The Mount Li Tomb, the burial place of Qin Shihuang (221-210 BC), the first emperor of a unified China, was built during his reign from 221 to 210 BC and is situated 40 km (25 miles) east of Xi'an, Shaanxi, China. The two walls surrounding the grave measure 2,173 x 974 m (7,129 x 3,195 ft) and 685 x 578 m (2,247 x 1,896 ft).

　　最大的独立陵墓，是骊山墓——秦始皇陵墓。位于中国西安以东 40 千米处，建造于公元前 221 ～公元前 220 年。围绕墓穴的两面墙的面积分别是 2,173 米 ×974 米和 685 米 ×578 米。

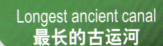

Longest ancient canal
最长的古运河

The longest canal in the ancient world was the Grand Canal of China from Beijing to Hangzhou. It was begun in 540 BC and not completed until 1327, by which time it extended (including canalized river sections) for 1,781 km (1,107 miles). Having been allowed by 1950 to silt up to the point that it was nowhere more than 1.8 m (6 ft) deep, it is now, however, piled by vessels of up to 2,000 tonnes.

最长的古运河，是从中国北京到杭州的京杭大运河。于公元前 540 年开凿，公元 1327 年完成，全长（包括河段）1,781 千米。

Largest ship launched sideways(transverse launch)
横向下水的自重最重的船舶

The MV *Hunte Stern*, 186 m (610 ft) long, 37,300 DWT chemical tanker built by Nanjing Jinling Shipyard, Nanjing, China, is the largest vessel ever to be launched transversely (sideways). At the time of its launch on 29th June 2003 it weighed 9,947 tonnes (22 million lb).

　横向下水的自重最重的船舶，长186 米，载重 37,300 吨，由中国南京金陵造船厂制造。2003 年 6 月 29 日下水，自重 9,947 吨。

Largest LED screen
最大的 LED 屏幕

The world's largest LED display screen measures 57 m wide by 63 m high (187 ft by 206 ft), with an area of 3,591 m² (38,653 ft²). It is located on the side of the office building of Aurora Ltd., Shanghai, China, and was completed in September 2003.

　最大的 LED 屏幕，是中国上海浦东震旦国际大楼外墙的 LED 屏幕，高 63 米，宽 57 米，面积 3,591 平方米。于 2003 年 9 月建造完成。

Longest bridge spanning open sea
最长的跨海大桥

Although not the longest bridge in the world, the bridge spanning the greatest width of open ocean is the 36 km (22.4 miles) long Hangzhou Bay Bridge linking the cities of Cixi and Haiyan in the Zhejiang Province of China. Construction on the $1.4 billion bridge began in June 2003 and was open to road traffic in May 2008.

　最长的跨海大桥，是中国的杭州湾大桥。位于中国浙江省，连接宁波慈溪和嘉兴海盐，全长 36 千米。2003 年 6 月开始修建，2008 年 5 月完工通车。↓

Longest bridge, span suspension bridge
最长的吊桥

With a main span of 1,377 m (4,517 ft), a width of 40 m (131 ft) and a length of 2.2 km (7,217 ft), the Tsing Ma Bridge in Hong Kong (China) is the world's longest span suspension bridge carrying both road and rail traffic. Its shipping clearance reaches 62 m (203 ft) and the tower height is 206 m (675 ft).

最长的吊桥，是中国香港的青马大桥。主跨长度 1,377 米，宽 40 米，长 2,200 米，是世界上行车、铁路双用的最长吊桥。该桥距海面 62 米，桥塔高度 206 米。↑

Longest bridge span for road and rail traffic
最长行车、铁路双用桥

The Qing Ma Bridge in Hong Kong, China, which opened to the public in May 1997, has a main span of 1,377 m (4,518 ft), making it the longest suspension-bridge span for combined road/railway traffic.

最长行车、铁路双用桥，是中国香港的青马大桥，主跨长度 1,377 米。于 1997 年 5 月投入使用。↑

47

航天员医

Longest maiden spaceflight
时间最长的太空首航

Of the three nations to launch humans into space to date, the longest maiden flight was achieved by China. On 15th October 2003, taikonaut Lieutenant Colonel Yang Liwei was sent into orbit on board the *Shenzhou 5* spacecraft on a mission which lasted 21 hours and 23 minutes from launch to touchdown.

时间最长的太空首航，是 2003 年 10 月 15 日，中国宇航员杨利伟创造的，他乘坐"神舟五号"飞船进入地球轨道。从发射到落地，飞行时间持续了 21 小时 23 分钟。

Smallest USB drive
最小的 USB 驱动器

In March 2006, ATP Taiwan announced they had created the Petito, the world's smallest USB flash drive, measuring 9.4 mm x 17.6 mm x 36.6 mm (0.37 in x 0.69 in x 1.42 in) and weighing 8 g (0.28 oz). The capacity ranges from 256 MB to 1 GB.

2006 年 3 月，ATP 台湾公司宣布他们研制出世界上最小的 USB 驱动器 Petito。体积为 9.4 毫米 ×17.6 毫米 ×36.6 毫米，重 8 克，存储容量为 256MB ～ 1GB。

Longest boom truck-mounted
最长的泵臂车

The longest boom of a truck-mounted concrete pump is 71.535 m (234 ft 8 in) long and was produced by SANY Heavy Industry Co., Ltd. in China, on 3rd August 2009. The multistage extensible arm is used in large scale engineering projects, in particular bridges, to pump concrete into the founding structures.

最长的泵臂车，泵臂架长 71.535 米。2009 年 8 月 3 日，由中国三一重工研制。

Largest revolving pedestal crane
最大的旋转式基座起重机

The revolving pedestal crane at the Yantai Raffles Shipyard in Yantai, China, is thought to be the most powerful of its kind. It can lift 2,000 tonnes (4.4 million lb) to a height of 95 m (311 ft) from its main hook, and 200 tonnes (441,000 lb) to 135 m (443 ft) from its secondary arm. The giant lifter sits atop a 40 m (131 ft) concrete tower and is designed for use in the construction of oil rigs and other tall vessels.

最大的旋转式基座起重机，是中国烟台莱佛士造船厂的旋转式基座起重机。主吊臂能把 2,000 吨的货物升至 95 米的高空，副吊臂能把 200 吨的货物升至 135 米。该起重机位于一座 40 米高的水泥台上，主要用来修建钻油台和其他大型船舶。

Oldest known paper
最早的纸

The oldest known piece of paper is thought to date from around 150 AD and was discovered in Wuwei in China's Gansu Province. It is made largely of cotton rags. Traditionally a court official called Cai Lun is credited with its invention around 100 AD.

最早的纸，被发现于中国甘肃省武威，大部分由棉花碎片组成。可约追溯至公元 150 年，传说由蔡伦发明。↓

Smallest commercially available hard drive
量产面市的最小硬盘

The world's smallest commercially available hard drive contains a disc just 2.5 cm (1 in) across. Of the models available in February 2004, the highest capacity was 2.2 GB and was manufactured by Magicstor Inc. (China).

量产面市的最小硬盘，由中国南方汇通微硬盘科技股份有限公司生产，其盘片直径为 2.5 厘米（1 英寸）。2004 年 2 月上市的该型号硬盘中，存储量最大的达 2.2GB。

Smallest model aircraft, radio controlled
最小的无线电遥控航行器模型

The smallest remotely controlled model aircraft has a wingspan of 132 mm (5.2 in) and was manufactured by the Shenzhen Yang Ri Electronics Co., Ltd. (China). It flew for three minutes in an office in Shenzhen, China, on 20th December 2007.

最小的无线电遥控航行器模型，由中国深圳阳日电子有限公司研制，翼展 132 毫米，于 2007 年 12 月 20 日，在中国深圳一间办公室内飞行了 3 分钟。

Smallest robot humanoid
最小的人形机器人

The smallest humanoid robot in production is the BeRobot, which measures 153 mm (6 in) high and is able to walk, kick and perform push-ups. The robot was manufactured by GeStream (Taiwan, China) and demonstrated at the Global SMEs Convention on 6th September 2007 in Kuala Lumpur, Malaysia.

最小的人形机器人 BeRobot，由台湾极趣科技股份有限公司制造，并于 2007 年 9 月 6 日在马来西亚吉隆坡的"国际中小型企业策略伙伴及商业网络贸易展"上展出。其身高 153 毫米，能走、踢和做俯卧撑。

Temple at the highest altitude
海拔最高的寺庙

The Rongbuk Monastery, between Tingri and Xigaze in Tibet, China, is at an altitude of approximately 5,100 m (16,732 ft), just 40 km (25 miles) from the Himalayas. It contains nine chapels, and a number of lamas and nuns live there.

海拔最高的寺庙，是绒布寺，位于中国西藏日喀则和定日之间，海拔 5,100 米，距珠穆朗玛峰仅 40 千米。↓

Tallest wooden pagoda
最高的木塔

The Sakyamuni Pagoda in Yingxian County of China's central Shanxi Province stands 65.86 m (216 ft) high and was constructed in 1056. The structure, which stands on a stone base and has five levels, is currently undergoing repairs after withstanding extreme weather, numerous earthquakes and even artillery fire during wartime.

最高的木塔，位于中国山西省应县，塔高 65.86 米，塔身共有五层，建成于 1056 年，建在一个石基座上。

Modern World

现代世界

现代世界
Modern World

Highest pilgrimage
海拔最高的朝圣地

The world's highest pilgrimage is the 53 km (33 mile) route on Mount Kailash (or Khang Rimpoche) in western Tibet, China, which is at an altitude of 6,714 m (22,028 ft). The Mountain is sacred to followers of Buddhism, Jainism, Hinduism and of the pre-Buddhist religion, Bonpo.

海拔最高的朝圣地，在中国西藏西部冈仁波齐峰（海拔 6,714 米）上，长达 53 千米。↓

Earliest written language
最早的书写语言

The earliest written language discovered has been on Yangshao culture pottery from Paa-t'o, found in 1962 near Xi'an in the Shaanxi province of China. This bears proto-characters for the numbers 5, 7 and 8 and has been dated to 5000-3000 BC.

最早的书写语言，是 1962 年在中国陕西省西安附近发现的仰韶文化陶器上刻写的符号，时间约为公元前 5000 ～公元前 3000 年。

Largest aluminium can of drink
最大的铝罐饮料

The largest aluminium can of drink had a volume of 8,460 litres (1,860 gal) and was made by the Vitalon Food Co., Ltd. (Taiwan, China) and displayed at the Chiang Kai-Shek Memorial Hall Plaza, Taipei, China, on 2nd June 2002.

最大的铝罐饮料，由台湾维他露食品股份有限公司生产，容量达 8,460 升。

Largest producer of meat (country)
最大的产肉国

In 2008, the world's largest producer of meat was China, with 72.69 million tonnes (160 billion) produced annually.

2008 年产肉量最多的国家，是中国，年产肉量达 7,269 万吨。

Largest shaving brush
最大的剃须刷

The largest shaving brush measured 26.5 cm (10.4 in) in height and was manufactured by Shenyang Delong Fur and Leather Products Co., Ltd. in Shenyang, China, on 20th July 2007.

最大的剃须刷，高 26.5 厘米。由中国沈阳德龙毛皮制品有限公司于 2007 年 7 月 20 日，在中国沈阳制造。

Largest set of room dividers
件数最多的一套屏风

The largest set of room dividers consists of 245 pieces and was verified in Beijing, China, on 17th October 2009. The ceramic paintings of A Dream of Red Mansions on the screens were painted by Pei Yongzhong (China).

件数最多的一套屏风，由 245 块屏风组成。屏风上的瓷板画《红楼梦》，由中国的裴永中绘制。↑

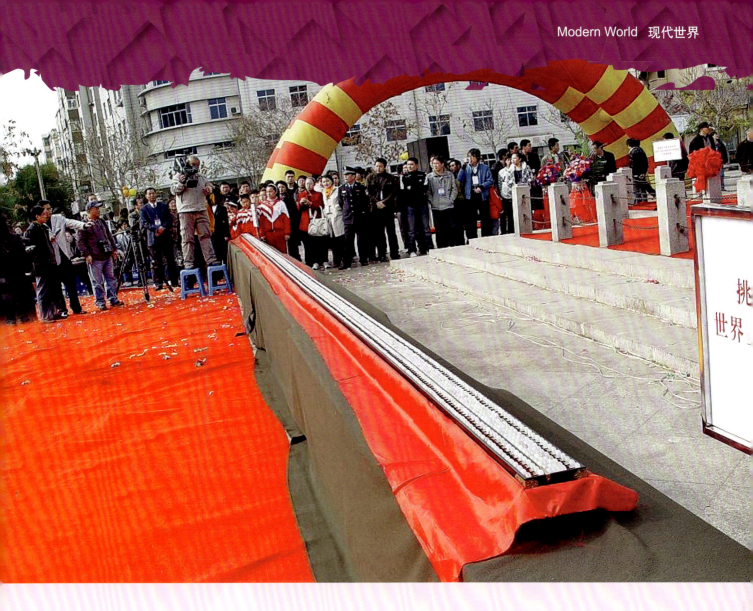

Longest abacus
最长的算盘

The longest abacus measures 13.11 m (43 ft 0.14 in) and was achieved at an event organized by the Development & Reform Commission of Fuxin Municipal Government in Fuxin City, Liaoning Province, China, on 25th October 2009.

最长的算盘，长 13.11 米。于 2009 年 10 月 25 日，在中国阜新由阜新市发展与改革委员会组织的活动中被认证。↑

Largest afforestation project
最大的造林工程

The world's largest afforestation project is the "Green Great Wall". A 4,480 km (2,783 mile) belt of forest is being created in northwest China in order to combat the encroaching threat of desertification and over-farming ruining vast areas of cultivated land. The project was initiated in 1978, and set to last until 2050 when a total of 35.6 million hectares (87.9 million acres) of land will be afforested. It is currently being coordinated by the State Forestry Administration of China. The total investment by the year 2000 was 3.6 billion yuan ($433 million). Another, smaller green belt is currently underway to protect the capital, Beijing. Desertification is extremely costly for the local and national economy, hence why China also holds the record for fastest reforestation.

最大的造林工程，是中国为了遏制沙漠化的威胁和过度开垦造成的大片耕地被毁的现状，在西北地区建造起的一条长4,480千米的森林带，被誉为"绿色长城"。该工程始于1978年，持续到2050年，造林总面积将达到3,560万公顷。

Largest bottle of cooking oil
最大的一瓶烹饪油

The largest bottle of cooking oil measures 5.12 m (16 ft 8 in) tall and contains 3,212 litres (706.54 gal) of camellia oil. It was verified at an event organized by the Pingyuan County Committee of the Communist Party of China and People's Government of Pingyuan County in Pingyuan County, Guangdong Province, China, on 28th September 2009.

最大的一瓶烹饪油，高5.12米，内装3,212升的茶籽油，于2009年9月28日，在中国广东省平远县被认证。↓

中国·广东·平远
Pingyuan Guangdong China
2009.9

Largest reforestation
最大规模的再造林工程

The Chinese State Forestry Administration announced in May 2002 the beginning of a 10-year reforestation project to plant up an area the size of Sweden. The replanted area, representing 5% of China's landmass, will measure about 440,000 km^2 (169,884 miles^2) and should offset some of the environmental problems caused by excessive logging in China over the past century. Recent updates from the Forestry Administration suggest that the programme is working, as targeted areas are experiencing an increase in annual average economic growth. In Jiangxi Province, for example, farmers' incomes from forestry increased by 41% year-on-year in 2005.

最大规模的再造林工程，是 2002 年 5 月由中国国家林业局宣布的十年再造林工程，计划造林面积将达到瑞典国土面积，占中国大陆面积的 5%，约 440,000 平方千米。

Largest porcelain bowl
最大的瓷碗

The largest bowl made of porcelain is 85.8 cm (2 ft 9.8 in) high and has an upper diameter of 202.5 cm (6 ft 7.7 in) and a bottom diameter of 109.6 cm (3 ft 7.15 in). The bowl was manufactured by Shenghong Group Co., Ltd. in Wujiang, China, on 6th June 2006.

最大的瓷碗，高 85.8 厘米，碗口直径 202.5 厘米，碗底直径 109.6 厘米。由中国江苏省吴江盛虹集团有限公司，于 2006 年 6 月 6 日烧制而成。↓

Largest Chinese almond cake
最大的中式杏仁饼

The largest Chinese almond cake weighed 155.2 kg (342 lb) and was made by Civil Aid Service Hong Kong (China) and displayed in Zhongshan, Guangdong, China, on 23rd March 2008.

最大的中式杏仁饼，重 155.2 千克。由中国香港民众安全服务队制作，于 2008 年 3 月 23 日，在中国广东省中山展示。

Largest cushion
最大的靠垫

The largest cushion is 10.08 m x 10.08 m (33 ft x 33 ft). It was made by Shanghai Konglong Textile Ornaments Co., Ltd. and was verified in Shanghai, China, on 29th May 2009.

最大的靠垫，规格为 10.08 米 ×10.08 米。由中国上海恐龙纺织装饰品有限公司制造，于 2009 年 5 月 29 日，在中国上海被认证。↓

Largest calligraphy brush
最大的毛笔

The largest calligraphy brush measured 5.6 m (18 ft 4 in) long, 2.06 m (6 ft 9 in) wide, and was used by calligrapher Zhang Kesi (China) to paint the Chinese character for "dragon" during a demonstration at the China International Horticultural Exposition, Shenyang, Liaoning Province, China, on 6th May 2006.

最大的毛笔，长 5.6 米，宽 2.06 米。属于中国书法家张克思，他于 2006 年 5 月 6 日，在辽宁省沈阳世界园艺博览会上，用它写下了汉字"龙"。

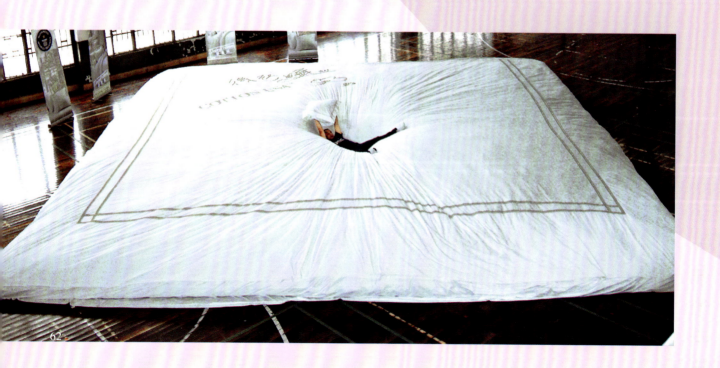

Largest dried bean curd
最大的豆腐干

The largest dried bean curd weighs 1,860 kg (4,100 lb) and was achieved by Sichuan Guozhu Bean Products Co., Ltd. in Yibin City, Nanxi County, China, on 26th October 2008.

最大的豆腐干，重 1,860 千克。2008 年 10 月 26 日，由中国四川省宜宾南溪县国砫豆制品有限公司创造该纪录。↑

Largest inkstone
最大的砚台

The largest inkstone measures 13.95 metres (45 ft 9 in) long, 3.44 metres (11 ft 3 in) wide and 1.55 metres (5 ft 1 in) high and is made from "Zicuishi" stone. It was created by Su Lihua (China) and was presented and measured in Ronggui Shunde, China, on 26th August 2009.

最大的砚台，长 13.95 米，宽 3.44 米，高 1.55 米，由中国的苏丽华制作，2009 年 8 月 26 日在中国广东省顺德测量。

Largest display of rice dumplings
规模最大的
粽子展

The largest display of rice dumplings contained 34,056 dumplings and was made by Towngas Rice Dumplings for the Community (China) at Hong Kong International Trade & Exhibition Centre in Hong Kong, China, on 10th June 2007.

　　规模最大的粽子展，于 2007 年 6 月 10 日，由中国香港中华煤气有限公司组织，在中国香港国际贸易展览中心举办，共展出 34,056 个粽子。

Largest diabolo
最大的空竹

The largest diabolo measured 1.3 m (4 ft 3 in) in diameter and was manufactured by Wang Yueqiu (China) and displayed on the set of *Zheng Da Zong Yi - Guinness World Records Special* in Beijing, China, on 20th September 2007.

　　最大的空竹，直径 1.3 米。由王跃秋制作，于 2007 年 9 月 20 日，在中国北京"正大综艺·吉尼斯中国之夜"节目中进行了展示。

Largest gong
最大的锣

The largest gong measures 5.15 m (16 ft 10 in) in diameter. It was made by Shanxi Baodi Real Estate Development Co., Ltd. and displayed at the Third China Taiyuan International Wheaten Food Festival, Shanxi Province, China, on 8th September 2005.

　　最大的锣，直径 5.15 米。由中国山西省宝地房地产开发公司制造，于 2005 年 9 月 8 日，在中国山西"第三届中国太原国际面食节"展出。←

Largest incense stick
最大的香

The largest incense stick (or joss stick) is 8.8 m (28 ft 10 in) tall, with a circumference of 74 cm (2 ft 5 in). It was constructed at the Palace Garden at Zhangmutou, Dongguan, Guangdong, China, and burned for 120 hours from 24th to 29th January 2004.

　　最大的香，高 8.8 米，周长 74 厘米。2004 年 1 月 24 ～ 29 日，在中国广东省东莞樟木头镇花园酒店焚烧达 120 小时。

见证仪式

童艺术剧院股份有限

Largest ice cream cake
最大的冰淇淋蛋糕

The record for the largest ice cream cake is 8,750 kg (19,290 lb) and was made by Beijing Allied Faxi Food Co., Ltd. for Beijing Children's Art Theater Co., Ltd. for the play *Amazing Mountain* and was displayed in Beijing, China, on 16th January 2006.

最大的冰淇淋蛋糕，重8,750千克。由中国北京艾莱发喜食品有限公司为北京儿童艺术剧院股份有限公司的儿童剧《魔山》制作，于2006年1月16日被认证并展示。↑

Largest jumper (sweater)
最大的毛线衫

The largest sweater had a chest measurement of 8.6 m (28 ft 2 in), a body length of 5 m (16 ft 4 in) and sleeve length of 4.3 m (14 ft 1 in) and was made by Dalang Woollen Trade Center (China) in Dongguan City, Guangdong Province, China, on 18th October 2007.

最大的毛线衫，胸围8.6米，身长5米，袖长4.3米。由中国大朗毛织贸易中心于2007年10月18日在中国广东省东莞创造该纪录。

Largest photo album
最大的相册

The largest photo album measures 4 m x 5 m (13 ft 1 in x 16 ft 4 in). It was created by Johnson's Baby China and unveiled in Beijing, China, on 10th June 2008.

　　最大的相册，规格为4米×5米。于2008年6月10日在中国北京亮相。↓

Largest spherical jigsaw puzzle
最大的球形拼图

The largest spherical jigsaw puzzle measures 4.77 m (15 ft 7.8 in) in circumference and was made by Unima Industrial (HK) Ltd. in Hong Kong, China. It was displayed and measured at the Hong Kong Convention and Exhibition Centre on 10th January 2005.

　　最大的球形拼图，周长4.77米。由中国香港优利玛实业（香港）有限公司研制，于2005年1月10日，在中国香港会议展览中心展出并测量。

Largest piece of tofu
最大的一块豆腐

The largest piece of bean curd weighed 3,120 kg (6,878 lb) and was made by Jiange County Government at Jianmenguan, Sichuan, China, on 28th September 2003.

最大的一块豆腐，重 3,120 千克。由中国四川省剑阁县政府于 2003 年 9 月 28 日在中国剑门关制作。←

Largest piggy bank
最大的猪形储蓄罐

The largest piggy bank is 5.6 m (18 ft 4 in) long, 3.96 m (12 ft 11 in) tall and has a circumference of 14.6 m (47 ft 10 in). The golden piggy bank, estimated to weigh 3 tons, was made by Zhong Xing Shenyang Commercial Building (Group) Co., Ltd. and unveiled in Shenyang, China, on 2nd May 2007.

最大的猪形储蓄罐，长 5.6 米，高 3.96 米，周长 14.6 米，重约 3 吨。由中国中兴沈阳商业大厦制作，于 2007 年 5 月 2 日亮相。↓

Largest toothpaste tube
最大的一管牙膏

The largest tube of toothpaste measures 2.957 m (9.7 ft) long and weighs 780 kg (1,719 lb). It was made for the Zhonghua toothpaste brand by Unilever in Shanghai, China, and was unveiled on 20th September 2005.

最大的一管牙膏，长 2.957 米，重 780 千克。由中国上海联合利华有限公司为中华品牌牙膏生产，于 2005 年 9 月 20 日亮相。◄

Largest rice dumpling
最大的粽子

The largest rice dumpling weighed 1,316 kg (2,901 lb 4 oz) and was made in Yunlin, Taiwan, China, on 25th April 2008.

最大的粽子，重 1,316 千克。于 2008 年 4 月 25 日，在台湾云林县制作完成。

Largest trolley case
最大的拉杆行李箱

The largest trolley case measures 175cm (5 ft 9 in) x 115 cm (3 ft 9.3 in) x 46 cm (1 ft 6.1 in) and was made by Shanghai Newest Luggage Co., Ltd. in Shanghai, China, during September 2006.

最大的拉杆行李箱，规格为 175 厘米 × 115 厘米 × 46 厘米。2006 年 9 月，由中国上海顶新箱包有限公司在上海制造。

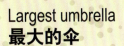

Largest umbrella
最大的伞

The largest umbrella measures 16.2 m (53 ft 2 in) in diameter and is 9.6 m (31 ft 6 in) tall. The umbrella was made by Sun City Umbrella Ind., Ltd. in Jinjiang City, Fujian Province, China, during October 2005.

　　最大的伞，直径 16.2 米，高 9.6 米。于 2005 年 10 月，由中国福建省晋江太阳城伞业有限公司制作。↓

Largest teapot
最大的茶壶

The largest ceramic teapot is 1.8 m (5 ft 10 in) in height and 1.5 m (4 ft 11 in) in diameter and was designed and fabricated by Xu Sanbao (China) in Yixing, Jiangsu Province, China, in February 2006, for Lu'an Guapian Tea Co., Ltd. of Anhui Province. The teapot is made of purple sand and can hold 10 kg (22 lb) of tea each time. The cover of the pot weighs 60 kg (132 lb).

　　最大的茶壶，高 1.8 米，直径 1.5 米。茶壶主体为紫砂烧制，每次泡茶可装 10 千克茶叶，仅茶壶盖就重 60 千克，是中国江苏省宜兴的徐三宝于 2006 年 2 月，为安徽省六安瓜片茶叶股份有限公司设计制造。

Largest collection of stamps featuring Olympic
收藏奥运邮票最多枚

The record for the largest collection of stamps featuring the Olympic Games belongs to Jin Feibao (China), with a total of 15,183 stamps, as of 10th December 2007, which he has been collecting since 2001.

　　收藏奥运邮票最多的人，是中国的金飞豹。自 2001 年起收藏奥运邮票，至 2007 年 12 月 10 日，共收藏 15,183 枚奥运邮票。↓

Largest wardrobe
最大的衣橱

The world's largest wardrobe is 4.57 m (15 ft) high, has three doors and was created by Majestic Furniture and Interior Design, Kowloon, Hong Kong, China, in February 2004.

　　最大的衣橱，高 4.57 米，有三个门。2004 年 2 月，由中国香港的皇室家居制造。

Longest gingerbread
最长的姜饼

The record for the longest gingerbread is 23.14 m (75 ft 10 in) and was achieved by the chefs of Langham Place Hotel in Mongkok, Hong Kong, China, on 3rd December 2005.

　　最长的姜饼，长 23.14 米。由中国香港朗豪酒店厨师于 2005 年 12 月 3 日制作。

Longest dancing dragon
最长的舞龙

The longest dancing dragon was 5,056 m (16,587 ft) long and was manufactured according to old traditions for the opening ceremony of the 25th Luoyang Peony Festival of Henan Province, China, on 10th April 2007.

　　最长的舞龙，长 5,056 米。是为 2007 年 4 月 10 日开幕的中国河南省洛阳牡丹花会庆典制作的。

Longest dragon lantern
最长的龙灯

The largest dragon lantern measured 277.2 m (909 ft 4 in) long from head to tail, 4.3 m (14 ft 1 in) high, and 2.51 m (8 ft 2 in) wide along its body, and was 13.9 m (45 ft 7 in) tall from the head to the ground. It was presented on 31st December 1999 as part of the celebrations at the Happy Valley Recreation Ground, Happy Valley, Hong Kong, China.

最长的龙灯，是由中国香港特别行政区政府和香港跑马协会制作的"千禧龙灯"。长 277.2 米, 高 4.3 米, 身宽 2.51 米，龙头距离地面 13.9 米。

Longest laundry chute
最长的洗衣店滑道

The Grand Hyatt Shanghai in Pudong, China, is the highest hotel in the world. It occupies floors 53 to 87 of the 88-storey Jin Mao Tower, the tallest building in China and one of the tallest buildings in the world. The hotel's laundry chute runs from the 87th floor to the basement of the Tower, a distance of around 330 m (1,083 ft), longer than the Eiffel Tower!

最长的洗衣店滑道，位于世界上最高的酒店——中国上海君悦大酒店内。该酒店位于国内最高建筑金茂大厦（共 88 层）的第 53 ~ 87 层。酒店的洗衣道从第 87 层通到地下室，长约 330 米，超过了埃菲尔铁塔的高度。

Longest golf cart
最长的高尔夫球车

The longest golf cart measures 6.68 m (21 ft 11 in) from bumper to bumper and was created by HSBC Champions. It was measured in Hong Kong, China, on 8th October 2008.

最长的高尔夫球车, 长 6.68 米。于 2008 年 10 月 8 日, 在中国香港测量，由"汇丰银行冠军赛"组织制作。↓

Largest collection of telephones
收藏电话机最多的人

Zhang Dafang (China) has collected 600 different telephones as of 20th April 2007, from all eras and from over the world for the past seven years.

收藏电话机最多的人，是中国的张大方，至 2007 年 4 月 20 日，共收集了不同时代世界各地的 600 个不同的电话机。

Largest cheerleading cheer
最大规模的啦啦队

The largest cheerleading cheer was achieved by 1,200 participants in the event "I'm lovin it When China Wins" at Beijing Olympic Sports Centre in Beijing, China, on 23rd April 2008.

最大规模的啦啦队，是 2008 年 4 月 23 日，由麦当劳公司在中国北京奥体中心组织的"我就喜欢中国赢"的活动中创造的，计有 1,200 人组成。↓

Largest collection of teapots
收藏茶壶最多的人

The largest collection of teapots belongs to Tang Yu (China) who has amassed 30,000 different teapots dated from the Song Dynasty (690-1279) to modern times since 1955.

收藏茶壶最多的人，是中国的唐玉（音）。自 1955 年开始，共收藏宋代至今的 30,000 个不同的茶壶。

世界紀錄博物館見証最多 3961 對雙胞

Largest gathering of twins
规模最大的双胞胎集会

The largest gathering of twins took place in Taiwan, China, when 3,961 pairs of twins converged on the square of Taipei City Hall on 12th November 1999.

　　规模最大的双胞胎集会，于1999年11月12日举行，共有3,961对双胞胎汇聚在台湾台北。↑

Largest display of lanterns
最大规模的
灯笼展

The largest display of lanterns in a single venue was 47,759 and was achieved by Tainan County Government at Solar City in the "Prayer for Peace" area of Tainan Science Park in Tainan, Taiwan, China, on 24th February 2008.

　　最大规模的灯笼展，于2008年2月24日，在台湾台南县科学园区的和平祈福灯区展出，共展出47,759只灯笼。

Largest gathering of Olympic mascots
最大规模的奥运吉祥物聚会

The largest gathering of Olympic mascots took place with 508 participants at Xinhua Square in Huhhot City, China, on 23rd June 2008. The event was organized by Inner Mongolia Yili Industrial Group Co., Ltd. and North News.

　　最大规模的奥运吉祥物聚会，于2008年6月23日，在中国内蒙古呼和浩特新华广场举办，共有508人参加。↑

Largest computer class
最大规模的计算机课程

The record for the largest computer class was 1,135 students and was set in the computer classroom of Shandong Lanxiang Senior Vestibule School in Jinan City, Shandong Province, China, on 15th January 2006.

　　最大规模的计算机课程，于2006年1月15日，在中国山东省济南蓝翔高级技工学校的计算机教室中举行，共有1,135名学生共同上课。

Largest gathering of dancing dragons
最大规模的舞龙

The largest gathering of dancing dragons consisted of 55 dragons and was set at the opening ceremony of the 25th Luoyang Peony Festival of Henan Province, China, on 10th April 2007.

　　最大规模的舞龙表演，于2007年4月10日，在中国河南省洛阳第25届牡丹花会开幕式上举行，共有55条舞龙参加表演。

Largest simultaneous balloon popping - single location
同一地点同时戳破气球的最多人数

The most people to pop a balloon simultaneously is 8,428, organized by The Marketing Store (Asia) Ltd. at the Talent Showcase 2005, Bo On Stadium, Shenzhen, China, on 18th March 2005.

　　2005 年 3 月 18 日，在中国深圳举行的"2005 才智展示"活动中，8,428 人同时参加戳破气球的活动，创造了同一地点同时戳破气球的最多人数的纪录。

Largest hot pot party
最大规模的火锅宴会

The largest hot pot party consisted of 13,612 people eating from 2,249 pots and was organized by the Chongqing Municipal People's Government in Chongqing, China, on 20th March 2007.

　　最大规模的火锅宴会，由中国重庆市人民政府组织，于 2007 年 3 月 20 日举办，创下了 13,612 人吃了 2,249 个火锅的纪录。↑

Largest parade of motorcycles with sidecars
最大规模的侧三轮摩托车巡游

A parade of 317 motorcycles and sidecars took place at Beijing Goldenport International Motor Park, Beijing, China, on 13th June 2004. The event was organized by Bullfroggies Beijing Sidecar Club.

　　2004 年 6 月 13 日，中国北京牛蛙摩托车俱乐部在北京金港国际汽车公园，举行了最大规模的侧三轮摩托车巡游，共有 317 辆侧三轮摩托车参加游行活动。

Largest collection of snow globes
收藏雪景玻璃球
最多的人

Wendy Suen (China) has 1,888 different snow globes, as of 7th April 2008, that she has collected since 2000.

　　收藏雪景玻璃球最多的人，是中国的孙韵儿。自 2000 年开始，至 2008 年 4 月 7 日，共收藏了 1,888 种不同的雪景玻璃球。↓

Largest golf facility
最大的高尔夫球场

The largest golf facility is Mission Hills Golf Club, China, with twelve 18-hole courses fully operational in December 2006.

　　最大的高尔夫球场，是中国的观澜湖高尔夫球场，共有 12 个 18 洞球场。2006 年 12 月对外营业。→

Largest collection of playing card
收藏最多扑克牌的人

The record for the largest collection of playing cards belongs to Liu Fuchang (China), with 11,087 different sets, as of 1st November 2007.

　　收藏最多扑克牌的人，是中国的刘福长。至 2007 年 11 月 1 日，共收藏 11,087 副不同种类的扑克牌。

Largest collection of dinosaur eggs
收藏恐龙蛋最多

The world's largest collection of dinosaur eggs numbers 10,008 individual samples as of November 2004. It is held at the Heyuan Museum, Guangdong Province, China. All of the eggs come from the late Cretaceous period (89 - 65 million years ago) and include eggs from oviraptorid and duck-billed dinosaurs.

　　收藏恐龙蛋最多的博物馆，是中国广东省河源市博物馆。馆藏 10,008 枚恐龙蛋化石，均为白垩纪晚期的（8,900 万～6,500 万年前）鸭嘴恐龙和窃蛋龙化石。

Largest collection of millstones
收藏最多石磨的人

The largest collection of millstones belongs to He Hengde (China), who has amassed 39,052 since 2004. The record was verified in Zhongyuan Folk Customs Park in Dancheng County, Henan Province, China, on 10th July 2009.

　　收藏最多石磨的人，是中国的贺恒德。自2004年起，共收藏39,052块石磨。该纪录于2009年7月16日在中国河南省郸城县中原民俗园得到认证。

Largest skatepark
最大的滑板运动场

The largest skatepark is the SMP Skatepark which has an area of 13,700 m² (147,465 ft²). It was built by SMP Clothing, Chentou Construction and Convic Design and opened in Shanghai, China, on 6th October 2005.

最大的滑板运动场，位于 2005 年 10 月 6 日开始营业的中国上海 SMP 滑板公园内，面积 13,700 平方米。

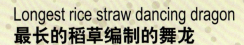

Longest rice straw dancing dragon
最长的稻草编制的舞龙

A rice straw dancing dragon made by Chen Dingfu, Chen Huanbing and Chen Huanjun (all China) in three months measured 200.8 m (658 ft 9 in) long from head to tail. Taking 126 people to operate, its first performance was at The Forth Leshan International Buddha Tour Day on 1st September 2002.

最长的稻草编制的舞龙，长 200.8 米。由陈鼎福等三名中国人用了 3 个月的时间制作，由 126 人舞动。↓

Largest racing club, non-profit
最大规模非营利赛马俱乐部

All money made by the Hong Kong Jockey Club, after payment of prizes, operating costs, betting tax and investments to improve racing and betting facilities, is donated to community projects, both social and educational. In 1998 the club donated more than $131.9 million, making it the biggest non-profit racing club ever.

1998 年中国香港赛马会向社区捐献了 1.319 亿美元，使其成为世界上最大规模的非营利赛马俱乐部。

Largest collection of clothing tags
收藏最多服装标签的人

Tao Chunlin (China) has a collection of 102,005 clothing tags that he has amassed since the 1970s.

收藏最多服装标签的人，是中国的陶春林。从 20 世纪 70 年代起，共收藏服装标签 102,005 件。↑

Longest chain of assembled robots
最长的组装机器人链

The longest chain of robots consisted of 255 four-legged robots assembled on the same day by the students of the Lingnan Dr. Zhong Rongguang Memorial Secondary School in Hong Kong, China, on 26th November 2006.

最长的组装机器人链，于 2006 年 11 月 26 日，由中国香港岭南钟荣光博士纪念中学的学生在同一天中用 255 个四脚机器人组装成。

Longest rice noodle
最长的米线

The longest rice noodle measured 548.7 m (1,800 ft 2 in) and was made by Council for Hakka Affairs Executive Yuan (Taiwan, China) at Taipei County Hakka Museum, Sansia, Taiwan, China, on 28th December 2008.

最长的米线，长 548.7 米。于 2008 年 12 月 28 日，由台湾"行政院"客家事务委员会在台北客家文化园区制作。

Largest collection of monkeys
收藏最多猴艺术品的人

Wang Lingxian (China) has 5,680 monkey items that she has collected since 1970.

收藏最多猴艺术品的人，是中国的王灵仙。自 1970 年起，共收藏 5,680 件猴子形象的艺术品。

Largest gathering of people dressed as sea animals
最大规模的人扮海洋动物集会

The largest gathering of people dressed as sea animals involved 5,590 participants for an event organized by People's Government of Putuo District, in Shenjiamen Fishing Harbor, Putuo District, Zhoushan City, Zhejiang Province, China, on 10th August 2007.

最大规模的人扮海洋动物集会，于 2007 年 8 月 10 日，在中国浙江省舟山普陀区沈家门渔港举行，共有 5,590 人参加。

Largest gathering of opposite sex twins
最大规模的龙凤胎集会

Organized by the Taipei Twins Association, a total of 806 pairs of opposite sex fraternal twins gathered at Chung-Shan Hall, Taipei, Taiwan, China, on 10th November 2002.

最大规模的龙凤胎集会，于 2002 年 11 月 10 日举行，共有 806 对龙凤胎汇聚在台湾台北。

Longest lanyard
最长的系索

The Hong Kong Girl Guides Association created the world's longest lanyard measuring 2,871 m (9,419.29 ft) starting in May 1999 and finishing on 27th February 2000 at the Mongkok Stadium in Hong Kong, China.

最长的系索，长 2,871 米。于 1999 年 5 月开始至 2000 年 2 月 27 日，由中国香港女童军总会在中国香港旺角大球场创造。

Longest sesame twist
最长的麻花

The longest sesame twist measured 2.66 m (8 ft 8 in) long and was made by the Laoliushi Fried Dough Twist General Store in Daying, Shaanxian, Henan, China, on 27th September 2001.

最长的麻花，长 2.66 米。于 2007 年 9 月 27 日，由中国河南省陕县大营镇的老刘氏麻花加工公司制作。

Most varieties of rum commercially available
商业销售的种类最多的朗姆酒

The record for the most varieties of rum commercially available is 102 and was set by Marco Polo Hong Kong Hotel. It was verified in Hong Kong, China, on 29th October 2008.

　　商业销售的种类最多的朗姆酒，共102种。由中国马可波罗香港酒店创造，于2008年10月29日，在中国香港认证。↑

Most people to visit a department store in one day
百货公司最大日客流量

The largest number of visitors to a single department store in one day is an estimated 1.07 million to the Nextage Shanghai, Shanghai, China, on 20th December 1995.

　　百货公司最大日客流量，是107万人。该纪录于1995年12月20日，由中国上海第一八佰伴百货公司创造。

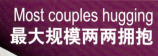

Most couples hugging
最大规模两两拥抱

The most couples hugging simultaneously is 3,009 at event organized by Hangzhou Tingjin FOOD CO., LTD. in Shanghai, China, on 26th August 2009.

最大规模两两拥抱，由中国杭州顶津食品有限公司组织，2009 年 8 月 26 日，在中国上海举行。创造了 3,009 对人同时拥抱的全新世界纪录。↓

Most densely populated island
人口最密集的岛屿

The world's most densely populated island is Ap Lei Chau, off the southwest coast of Hong Kong Island. Ap Lei Chau has a population of 80,000 who are living in an area measuring 1.3 km² (0.5 miles²). The actual population density, therefore, is 60,000 per 1 km² (160,000 per 1 mile²).

人口最密集的岛屿，是中国香港岛西南边的鸭脷洲。面积 1.3 平方千米，居住了 80,000 人，人口密度为每平方千米 60,000 人。

Most people hula hooping
最多人同时转呼拉圈

The record for the most people hula-hooping simultaneously is 2,290 and was set during an event organized by China Food GMP Development Association and the Bureau of Health, Kaohsiung City Government on 28th October 2000 at Chung Cheng Stadium, Kaohsiung City, Taiwan, China.

最多人同时转呼拉圈的纪录，于 2000 年 10 月 28 日，在台湾创造，共有 2,290 人参加。

Most expensive diamond rough cut
最昂贵的天然钻石

Most people painting each other's faces simultaneously
最多人同时
互相涂抹脸

The highest price known to be paid for a rough diamond was £5.8 million ($9.9 million) for a 255.10 carat stone from Guinea, paid by the William Goldberg Diamond Corporation in partnership with the Chow Tai Fook Jewellery Co., Ltd. of Hong Kong, China, in March 1989. Many sales of polished diamonds are considered private transactions, and the prices paid not disclosed.

最昂贵的天然钻石，是中国香港的周大福珠宝行及 William Goldberg 珠宝公司，于 1989 年以 580 万英镑（990 万美元）购买的一颗来自几内亚的 255.10 克拉的天然钻石。这是天然钻石卖出的最高价。

The most people painting each other's faces simultaneously in one location was achieved by 13,413 participants at an event organized by the People's Government of Qiubei County at Jiaolian Square in Qiubei County, Yunnan Province, China, on 15th August 2009.

最多人同时互相涂抹脸的活动，于 2009 年 8 月 15 日，在中国云南省丘北县椒莲广场举行，共有 13,413 人参加。↓

Most people playing wood block/ Chinese block
最多人数 演奏响木

The record for the most people playing wood block/Chinese block was achieved by 240 participants at the Ang Ping Buddha's Birthday Celebration in Hong Kong, China, on 11th May 2008.

最多人数演奏响木的纪录，于 2008 年 5 月 11 日，在中国香港昂坪创造，共有 240 人参加。

Most expensive bathroom
最昂贵的洗手间

Jeweller Lam Sai-wing built a HK$27 million ($3.5 million) washroom in his Hong Kong shop made entirely out of gold and precious jewels. The toilet bowls, wash basins, toilet brushes, toilet paper holders, mirror frames, wall mounted chandeliers, wall tiles and doors are all made out of solid 24-carat gold. The ceiling is decorated with ruby, sapphire, emerald and amber and even the floor to the washroom is embedded with 900 g (2 lb) gold bars.

最昂贵的洗手间，是中国珠宝商林世荣在其中国香港的店里用黄金和珠宝建造的，价值 2,700 万港币（350 万美元）。其抽水马桶、盥洗池、盥洗刷、卫生纸盒、镜框、墙上的装饰灯、瓷砖、门都是用 24K 金制成。天花板用红宝石、蓝宝石、绿宝石和琥珀装饰。门到洗手间的地板都是用 900 克金条嵌入的。

Most gender specific language
最具性别特征的 文字

For about 1,000 years in a region of the Hunan province, China, *nüshu* ("women's writing") has been used exclusively by women to communicate their deeper feelings to other women. It is thought that it was invented by the concubine who belonged to an emperor of the Song Dynasty (960-1279).

最具性别特征的文字，是女书。这是在中国湖南省的一个地区近千年来只被妇女使用的一种文字，用于妇女之间表达情感。据说这种文字是由宋朝（960 ～ 1279 年）一个皇帝的妃子发明的。

Oldest bowl of noodles
最古老的一碗面条

In October 2005, the world's oldest bowl of noodles was uncovered by archaeologists working at the Lajia archaeological site in northwestern China. The thin, yellow noodles (made from millet) were preserved under an upturned bowl, 3 m (10 ft) below the surface and have been aged to 4,000 years old!

最古老的一碗面条，于 2005 年 10 月被考古学家们在中国西安发现。这碗面条看起来细细黄黄的，由小米面做成，在地表下 3 米处保存了约 4,000 年。

Most postcards sent from a single location at one time
同一地点同时寄出的最多明信片

The most postcards sent from one location at one time is 4,493 and was set for China 2009 World Stamp Exhibition in Luoyang City, China, on 10th April 2009.

同一地点同时寄出最多明信片的纪录，于 2009 年 4 月 10 日，在中国洛阳"中国 2009 世界集邮展览"上创出，共寄出 4,493 张明信片。↓

Most TV sets in one country
电视机最多的国家

The country with the most televisions is China, which had 400 million TV sets in 1997.

拥有电视机最多的国家，是中国。1997 年拥有 4 亿台电视机。

Most primary schools in one country
小学最多的国家

The country with the greatest number of primary schools is China, with 849,123 in 1997.

拥有小学最多的国家，是中国。1997 年拥有 849,123 所小学。

Most hospitals in one country
医院最多的国家

The country with the greatest number of hospitals is China, with 67,807 in 1995.

拥有医院最多的国家，是中国。1995 年拥有 67,807 所医院。

Most pharmacists in one country
药剂师最多的国家

The country with the greatest number of pharmacists is China, with 418,000 in 1995.

拥有药剂师最多的国家，是中国。1995 年拥有药剂师 418,000 人。

The country with most physicians
内科医生最多的国家

The country with the greatest number of physicians is China, which had 1,918,000 in 1995, including dentists and those practising traditional Chinese medicine.

拥有内科医生最多的国家，是中国。1995 年达 1,918,000 人，包括牙医和中医。

Most remote city from the sea
离海最远的城市

The city most remote from the sea is Urumqi, the capital of China's Xinjiang Uygur Autonomous Region, which lies at a distance of about 2,500 km (1,553 miles) from the nearest coastline.

离海最远的城市，是中国新疆维吾尔自治区首府乌鲁木齐，距它最近的海岸在 2,500 千米外。

Smallest commercial jigsaw puzzle
商业销售的最小拼图

The smallest commercially available 1,000 pieces jigsaw puzzle is manufactured by Standard Project Limited who produce Tomax puzzles in Hong Kong, China. It measures 297 x 420 mm (11.69 x 16.53 in). The miniature puzzles were launched in 2003 and depict various designs, with images ranging from landmarks to famous works of art.

商业销售的最小拼图，有 1,000 块，尺寸为 297 毫米 ×420 毫米，图案涉及著名景点和艺术名画，由中国香港平建有限公司 (Standard Project Limited) 生产，2003 年投放市场。

Smallest model helicopter, remote controlled
最小的遥控 直升机模型

The smallest remote-controlled model helicopter is the PicooZ MX-1 by Silverlit Toys Manufactory Ltd. (Hong Kong, China). It weighs 8 g (0.28 oz) and was manufactured in Causeway Bay, Hong Kong, China.

最小的遥控直升机模型为 PicooZ MX-1，重 8 克。由中国香港银辉玩具制品厂生产。↑

Tallest stilts
最高的高跷

The tallest stilts ever mastered measured 16.41 m (53 ft 10 in) from ground to ankle. Saimaiti Yiming (China) was able to walk a distance of 10 steps on them, without touching his safety lines, in Shanshan County, Xinjiang, China, on 15th November 2006.

最高的高跷，长 16.41 米（从地面到脚踝）。于 2006 年 11 月 15 日，由中国的赛买提·依明在中国新疆鄯善县踩着走了 10 步。

Tallest flower arrangement/structure
最高的花卉楼

The tallest flower structure was the Chrysanthemum tower "Tengwangge", measuring 24.43 m (80 ft 1 in) high. It was created for the 9th China (Xiaolan, Zhongshan) Chrysanthemum Exhibition in Xiaolan town, China, and measured on 23rd November 2007.

最高的花卉楼，高 24.43 米。是 2007 年 11 月 23 日，在第九届中国（中山小榄）菊花展览会上展出的菊花楼"滕王阁"。↓

Tallest vase
最高的花瓶

The tallest vase is a twin-mouth vase made of porcelain clay standing 6.68 m (21.9 ft) high. It was constructed at the Shui-Li Snake Kiln Ceramics Cultural Park, Ting Kan Village, Taiwan, China, over a period of six months and finished on 10th June 2000.

最高的花瓶，是瓷土制的双口花瓶，高 6.68 米。历时 6 个月，于 2000 年 6 月 10 日完工，立在台湾南投水里蛇窑陶艺文化园。

Arts and Media

艺术与媒体

Longest commercially made film - general cinema release
电影院公开上映的最长的商业影片

The Burning of the Red Lotus Temple (China, 1928-1931), adapted by the Star Film Co. from a newspaper serial *Strange Tales of the Adventurer in the Wild Country* by Shang K'ai-jan, was released in 18 feature-length parts over a period of three years. Although never shown publicly in its 27 hour entirety, some cinemas put on all-day performances of half-dozen parts in sequence.

电影院公开上映的最长的商业影片，是根据中国平江不肖生的武侠小说《江湖奇侠传》改编，由中国明星影片公司摄制的电影《火烧红莲寺》。于 1928 ～ 1931 年，三年内连续拍出了 18 集，全长 27 小时。

Highest box office film gross for a Chinese film
最高票房的中国电影

Ying Xiong (*Hero*) China, 2002, $169 million, Director Zhang Yimou (China).

最高票房的中国电影，是中国的张艺谋导演的《英雄》，创造了 2002 年 1.69 亿美元的票房收入。←

Longest first-run of a film in one cinema
在同一电影院首映时间最长的电影

Romance in Lushan (China, 1980) first opened at the Jiangxi Movie Circulation and Screening Company, Lushan, China, on 12th July 1980 and has been shown daily four times a day since then.

在同一电影院首映时间最长的电影，是中国电影《庐山恋》。自 1980 年 7 月 12 日开始，在中国庐山由江西电影发行放映公司放映，每日 4 场，直至今天。→

Largest carved jade item
最大的玉雕

The largest statue of Buddha made from a single piece of jade weighs 260.76 tonnes (574,876 lb 11 oz) and measures 7.95 m (26 ft) high, 6.88 m (22 ft 6.8 in) wide and 4.1 m (13 ft 5.4 in) deep. It is found within a temple at the Jade Buddha Garden, Anshan, Liaoning Province, China.

　　最大的玉雕，是由一整块玉雕成的一尊佛像，重 260.76 吨，高 7.95 米，宽 6.88 米，厚 4.1 米，现存放于中国辽宁省鞍山玉佛苑的一个寺庙中。

Largest origami mosaic
最大的折纸拼图

The largest origami mosaic is 320.87 m² (3,453 ft²) and was created by Hong Kong Youth Visual Art Association, Hong Kong Chinese Arts Festival, Lo Fung Art Gallery Ltd. and Hong Kong Union of Visual Artists Limited, at Hiu Kwong Street Sports Centre, in Kwun Tong, Hong Kong, China, on 26th July 2008.

　　最大的折纸拼图，面积为 320.87 平方米。于 2008 年 7 月 26 日，在中国香港观塘晓光街体育馆摆出。↓

Longest-running film series
延续时间最长的电影系列片

The longest-running film series are the 103 features made in Hong Kong, China, about the 19th century martial arts hero Huang Fei-Hong, starting with *The True Story of Huang Fei-Hong* (1949) and continuing to the latest production, *Lion in the West of Huang Fei-hong* (1997), a total of 48 years.

　　延续时间最长的电影系列片，是在中国香港制作的 19 世纪武术英雄黄飞鸿系列，共有 103 集。最早的一部是 1949 年的《黄飞鸿正传》，最后一部是 1997 年的《黄飞鸿之五：西域雄狮》，延续时间达 48 年。

Largest hotel mural
最大的酒店壁画

The Great Motherland of China, a Chinese landscape mural in the Island Shangri-La Hotel in Hong Kong, China, measures 50 m x 15.24 m (164 ft x 50 ft) and is 16 stories high. It can be viewed from a glass elevator between the 41st and the 56th floors.

　　最大的酒店壁画，是中国香港香格里拉酒店的一幅名为《大好河山》的巨型中国山水壁画，规格为 50 米 ×15.24 米，有 16 层楼高。

93

Largest ceramic mosaic
最大的陶瓷拼图

The largest ceramic mosaic is 200.87 m (659 ft) long and 7.44 m (24 ft 4 in) tall and represents a scaled up reproduction of a famous Chinese painting by Song Dynasty (960-1279) artist, Zhang Zeduan. The mosaic is owned by Shiyitang Pharmaceutical Factory of Harbin Pharmaceutical Group in Harbin City, Heilongjiang Province, China, and was completed in August 2006.

最大的陶瓷拼图，长200.87米，高7.44米，是表现中国宋代著名艺术家张择端的一幅名画。由中国黑龙江省哈尔滨哈药集团世一堂制药厂制作，完成于2006年8月。

Largest shuttlecock mosaic
最大的羽毛球拼图

The largest shuttlecock mosaic measures 30.375 m² (326.95 ft²) and was created by Zhao Fuqiang (China) on 2nd August 2009. It was comprised of 5,236 shuttlecocks and depicted two interlaced hearts and the words "Show the love with shuttlecocks, be together forever".

最大的羽毛球拼图，面积达30.375平方米，由5,236个羽毛球组成，拼成两个互相交叉的心和"羽球传情　永结同心"八个字。该纪录由中国的赵富强于2009年8月2日创造。↓

Largest fruit mosaic
最大的水果拼图

The largest fruit mosaic consisted of 372,525 fruits, measured 2,220 m² (23,895.79 ft²) and was created for the Fourth Navel Orange Tourism Festival of Pingyuan County by the Pingyuan County Committee of the Communist Party of China and People's Government of Pingyuan County in Pingyuan County, Guangdong Province, China, on 1st December 2008.

最大的水果拼图，面积为2,220平方米，由372,525个水果组成。2008年12月1日，在中国广东省平远县第四届脐橙旅游节上创造。

Largest button mosaic
最大的纽扣拼图

The largest button mosaic measured 66.89 m² (720 ft²), contained 296,981 buttons and was made at Maritime Square, Tsing Yi District, Hong Kong, China, for the "Springroll Love Mosaic" project between 23rd and 28th July 2006.

最大的纽扣拼图，面积 66.89 平方米，含 296,981 个纽扣。2006 年 7 月 28 日，由中国香港青衣区青衣城制作。

Largest permanent light and sound show
最大型灯光音乐汇演

The world's largest permanent light and sound show comprises 33 buildings and is staged every night at Victoria Harbour in Hong Kong, China. The show, entitled "A Symphony of Lights", was developed by the Tourism Commission of the Government of the Hong Kong Special Administrative Region and was launched on 17th January 2004.

最大型灯光音乐汇演，名为"幻彩咏香江"。由中国香港旅游发展局发起，2004 年 1 月 17 日启用。33 幢建筑物于每晚同一时段，以互动灯光及音乐效果展现维多利亚港夜景。↓

Largest revolving stage
最大的旋转舞台

The largest revolving stage measured 10 m x 9.44 m (32 ft 10 in x 31 ft) and was used by Aaron Kwok (Hong Kong, China) for the Aaron Kwok De Show Reel Extension Live Concert at the Asia World Arena, Hong Kong, China, on 17th February 2008.

最大的旋转舞台，面积为 10 米 ×9.44 米。是 2008 年 2 月 17 日，由中国的郭富城在中国香港 Asia World Arena 举办"郭富城舞林正传演唱会"时使用的。

Largest simultaneous percussion performance
最大规模同时表演的打击乐

The largest percussion performance was held at the Hong Kong Coliseum, Hong Kong, China, on 2nd July 2002 when 10,102 people played a percussive rhythm for over six minutes.

最大规模同时表演的打击乐，2002 年 7 月 2 日在中国香港体育馆举行，10,102 人按同一个节奏同时表演 6 分钟。

Largest drum ensemble
最大规模的鼓乐表演

The record for the largest drum ensemble is 10,045 drummers, and was achieved by the Hong Kong Federation of Youth Groups (China), at the Hong Kong Coliseum in Hong Kong, China, on 29th June 2007.

最大规模的鼓乐表演，2007 年 6 月 29 日，由中国香港青年协会组织，在中国香港体育馆举行，有 10,045 名鼓手参加表演。

Largest recorder ensemble
最大规模的牧笛合奏

The largest recorder ensemble involved 6,243 participants at an event organized by Hang Seng Bank at the Hong Kong Exhibition Centre, Wanchai, Hong Kong, China, on 27th December 2004.

　　最大规模的牧笛合奏，2004 年 12 月 27 日，由中国恒生银行组织，在中国香港湾仔会议展览中心举行，有 6,243 人参加表演。

Largest *erhu* ensemble
最大规模的二胡合奏

The largest *erhu* ensemble consisted of 1,490 musicians and was organized on the occasion of the First Xuzhou - China International Huqin Festival at Xuzhou Stadium, Jiangsu Province, China, on 17th October 2004.

　　最大规模的二胡合奏，是 2004 年 10 月 17 日，由 1,490 人在中国江苏省徐州体育馆举办的"首届国际胡琴艺术节"上同时演奏的二胡曲目。 ↑↓

Largest flute
最大的笛子

The largest playable flute is 3.25 m (10.66 ft) long and 5 cm (1.97 in) in diameter and was made by Fushun Youth and Children Palace. It was verified in Fushun City, Liaoning Province, China, on 14th July 2009.

　　最大的笛子,长3.25米,直径5厘米,可演奏。由中国抚顺市少年宫创造,2009年7月14日在中国辽宁省抚顺被认证。↑

Largest flute ensemble
最大规模的笛子合奏

The largest flute ensemble was achieved by 1,975 participants in Fushun City, Liaoning Province, China, on 14th July 2009. The event was organized by Fushun Youth and Children Palace.

　　最大规模的笛子合奏,2009年7月14日,由中国抚顺市青少年宫组织,在辽宁省抚顺举行,有1,975人参加表演。↑

Largest *guzheng* ensemble
最大规模的古筝合奏

The largest *guzheng* ensemble consisted of 2,348 participants at an event in Longwan Seaside Square in Huludao City, Liaoning Province, China, on 8th August 2007. The event was organized by Huludao Municipal Committee of the CPC and Huludao Municipal Government (both China).

　　最大规模的古筝合奏，2007 年 8 月 8 日，在中国辽宁省葫芦岛龙湾海滨广场举行，有 2,348 名古筝手表演。↑

Largest handprint painting
最大的手印画

The largest handprint painting measures 3,195.2 m² (34,392.71 ft²) and was achieved by an event organized by China Communist Youth League Dongguan Committee and GuanShan BiShui Richwood in Dongguan, Guangdong Province, China, on 25th July 2009.

　　最大的手印画，面积为 3,195.2 平方米。于 2009 年 7 月 25 日，由中国东莞市团委与丰泰观山碧水在东莞主办的活动中创造。←

Largest bead mosaic
最大的串珠拼图

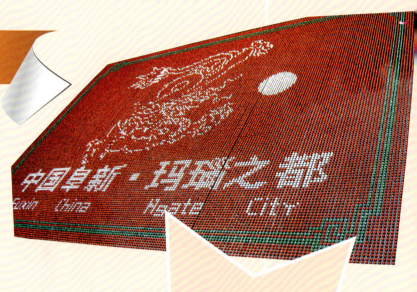

The largest bead mosaic measures 6.72 m² (72.33 ft²) and was achieved by Cao Zhitao (China) at an event organized by the Development & Reform Commission of Fuxin Municipal Government in Fuxin City, Liaoning Province, China, on 25th October 2009.

　　最大的串珠拼图，面积为 6.72 平方米。是中国的曹志涛于 2009 年 10 月 25 日，在中国阜新由阜新市发展与改革委员会组织的一个活动中制作的。→

Longest chain of beads
最长的串珠链

The longest chain of beads measured 122.6 m (402 ft 2.76 in) and was achieved at an event organized by the Development & Reform Commission of Fuxin Municipal Government in Fuxin City, Liaoning Province, China, on 25th October 2009.

　　最长的串珠链，长 122.6 米。于 2009 年 10 月 25 日，在中国阜新由阜新市发展与改革委员会组织的一个活动中被认证。→

Largest finger painting
最大的手指画

The largest finger painting was achieved by 3,242 students at an event organized by the Organizing Committee of Anti Youth Drug Abuse Campaign at Victoria Park in Hong Kong, China, on 26th November 2009. It measures 2,101.43 m² (22,619.51 ft²).

　　最大的手指画，面积为 2,101.43 平方米。是由 3,242 名学生于 2009 年 11 月 26 日，在中国香港的维多利亚公园创造的，此活动是禁毒宣传教育活动之一。←

Largest *matouqin* ensemble
最大规模的马头琴合奏

The record for the largest ensemble of *matouqin* consisted of 2008 musicians and was set in Qian Gorlos Mongolian Autonomous County, Songyuan City, Jilin Province, China, on 15th July 2008.

最大规模的马头琴合奏，2008 年 7 月 15 日，在中国吉林省松原前郭尔罗斯蒙古族自治县举行，有 2,008 名演员参加表演。→

Largest spoon ensemble
最大规模的勺子合奏

The largest spoon ensemble featured 888 participants playing along to the *William Tell Overture* conducted by Tang-ChiChung (China) at the Civil Aid Service Headquarters, Hong Kong, China, on 6th July 2009.

最大规模的勺子合奏，是 2009 年 7 月 6 日，由 888 人在中国香港用勺子演奏的《威廉·泰尔序曲》。

Largest tambourine ensemble
最大规模的手鼓合奏

The largest tambourine ensemble was achieved by 9,902 participants in an event organized by Taipei County Government in Taipei, Taiwan, China, on 1st January 2008.

最大规模的手鼓合奏，2008 年 1 月 1 日，在台湾台北举行，有 9,902 人参加表演。

Longest marathon karaoke by multiple participants
最长时间的多人马拉松卡拉 OK 连唱

The longest karaoke marathon by multiple participants lasted for 456 hr 2 min and 5 sec in an event organized by New Culture View in Changchun City, China, between 20th February and 11th March 2009.

最长时间的多人马拉松卡拉 OK 连唱，在中国长春《新文化报》组织的多人连唱卡拉 OK 活动中创造，自 2009 年 2 月 20 日至 3 月 11 日，共持续 456 小时 2 分 5 秒。←↓

Largest *xun* ensemble
最大规模的埙合奏

The largest *xun* ensemble involved 11,551 participants at Jhong Jheng Stadium, Kaohsiung City, Taiwan, China, on 18th December 2004.

最大规模的埙合奏，2004 年 12 月 18 日，在台湾高雄举行，有 11,551 人参加表演。

Largest snow sculpture/structure
最大的雪雕／建筑

The largest snow sculpture, entitled "Romantic Feelings" measured 35 m (115 ft) tall and 200 m (656 ft) long when it was created as part of the annual Harbin International Ice and Snow Sculpture Festival, which opened in the Heilongjiang Province, China, on 20th December 2007. A team of 600 sculptors from 40 different countries used 3,398 m^3 (120,000 ft^3) of snow to create the Olympic themed landscape, which included a French cathedral, an ice maiden and a Russian church.

最大的雪雕／建筑，名为"浪漫风情"，高 35 米，长 200 米，用雪 3,398 立方米，是 2007 年 12 月 20 日在中国开幕的"哈尔滨国际冰雪雕塑节"上的一部分雪雕。

Largest stone sculpture
最大的石雕

The statue of the God of Longevity is the largest stone carving measuring 200 m (656 ft) wide and 218 m (715 ft) high and is on the northwest side of the peak, Guimeng, in the Mengshan Mountains near Pingyi, Shandong, China.

最大的石雕，名为"寿星"，高 218 米，宽 200 米。位于中国山东省平邑县附近的蒙山主峰龟蒙的西北侧。

Largest stone mosaic
最大的石头拼图

On 29th July 2001 the heart Chorus - a team of 2001 students, teachers and parents - completed the world's largest stone mosaic with a total surface area of 4,720 m^2 (50,805.65 ft^2) in the Luozuling Park, Shiyan Town of Shenzhen, China. The event was organized by HK Talent Foundation Ltd. and HK United Youth Association Ltd.

最大的石头拼图，总面积达 4,720 平方米。于 2001 年 7 月 29 日，在中国深圳石岩镇的罗租岭公园，由 2,001 名来自全国各地的中小学生、教师和家长组成的"心连心"团队共同完成。

Largest painting by numbers
最大的填色画

The largest painting by numbers measures 2,461.3 m²
(26,493.11 ft²) and was created by 960 students from
Mingren Primary School at an event organized by *Kerchin
Metropolis Newspaper* in Tongliao City, Inner Mongolia
Autonomous Region, China, on 30th September 2009.

最大的填色画，面积为 2,461.3 平方米。由中国内蒙
古明仁小学的 960 名学生于 2009 年 9 月 30 日，在中国通
辽创造。↑

Most cinema
screens (country)
拥有电影银幕
最多的国家

According to the most
recent statistics, China
currently has 65,500 cinema
screens. As a comparison,
the USA has 35,280, India
11,962 and the UK 3,402.

拥有电影银幕最多
的国家，是中国，拥有
65,500 块电影银幕。

Largest para para dance
最大规模的帕拉帕纳舞

Organized by the Bauhinia Junior Chamber, a total of 840
people para para danced to the music "Fantasy" for over six
minutes at the Charter Road Pedestrian Precinct, Hong Kong,
China, on 17th June 2001. Para para is a dance style popular in
Asia and is a combination of line and club dancing with most
movement on the dance floor made with the hands.

最大规模的帕拉帕纳舞，2001 年 6 月 17 日，在中
国香港渣打路步行区表演，共有 840 人参加，众人随着
音乐跳了 6 分钟。

Most watched TV network
观众最多的电视台

The state-owned station China Central Television (CCTV) is transmitted to 90% of all viewers in China. It is estimated that more than 1.1 billion people have access to television in China. The single most watched show is the daily *Xin Wen Lian Bo* (News Hookup), which attracts 315 million viewers.

拥有观众最多的电视台，是中国的中央电视台。约有 11 亿观众，其中 3.15 亿观众收看中央电视台每天播出的《新闻联播》节目。→

Most watched national network TV broadcast
最多人收看的全国联播电视节目

The most watched national network TV broadcast in the world is China Central Television's New Year's Eve *Gala* (aka *Spring Festival*) broadcast which has regularly attracted viewing figures of over 300 million.

最多人收看的全国联播电视节目，是中国中央电视台的春节联欢晚会，大约有 3 亿以上观众观看。

Most people performing sign language
最多人参加的手语表演

The most people performing sign language simultaneously to the same song is 4,796 and was organized by *Zheng Da Zong Yi* of CCTV and Zhuhai Campus of Beijing Institute of Technology in Zhuhai City, Guangdong Province, China, on 10th January 2007.

最多人参加的手语表演，是 2007 年 1 月 10 日，由中国中央电视台《正大综艺》节目和北京理工大学珠海校区（广东省珠海）共同组织，4,796 人伴随同一首歌进行的手语表演。↑→

Most autographs prints signed continuously
连续在印刷品上签名的最多个数

Chinese-American watercolour artist Zeng Jingwen personally signed 120,000 copies of 12 of his lithographed paintings in 12 days of continuous sitting in Hong Kong, China, from 8th to 19th May 1980.

连续在印刷品上签名的最多个数纪录，由华裔水彩画家曾景文创造。1980 年 5 月 8～19 日，曾景文连续 12 天在香港为他的 12 本水彩画印刷品签名，共签了 120,000 册。

Oldest band
年龄最大的乐队

The oldest band is the Peace Old Jazz band, composed of six veteran musicians, whose average age is 76 (as of November 2007). They have performed every night for over 20 years in Shanghai, China.

年龄最大的乐队，是中国上海和平饭店的老年爵士乐队。由6名老音乐家组成，平均年龄是76岁（截至2007年11月）。20多年来，他们每晚都在中国上海表演。

Oldest opera singer
年龄最大的歌剧演员

Luo Pinchao (b. China, 19th June 1912), who began his singing career in 1930, continues to regularly perform Cantonese Opera and celebrated his 93rd birthday and record-breaking career with a performance at the Guangdong Cantonese Opera Grand Artistic Theatre, Guangzhou, China, on 20th June 2004.

　　年龄最大的歌剧演员，是中国的罗品超。1912 年 6 月 19 日出生于中国，1930 年开始他的演唱生涯。从那时起，他经常性地演出粤剧。2004 年 6 月 20 日，他在中国广州友谊剧院庆祝他的 93 岁生日和破纪录的职业生涯。↓

Tallest stone Buddha
最高的石佛

The Leshan Giant Buddha in the Sichuan Province of China was carved out of a hillside in the 8th century and stands 71 m (233 ft), making it the tallest statue of Buddha to be carved entirely out of stone. The statue and surrounding area have been designated a World Heritage Site by UNESCO.

　　最高的石佛，是中国四川省的乐山大佛，高 71 米，于公元 8 世纪由山体的一侧雕凿而成。佛像和其周围区域被联合国教科文组织列为世界遗产。→

Talented People and Feats

奇人与奇技

Furthest distance flipping a two kg weight with the stomach
丹田弹 2 千克重物的最远距离

The furthest distance achieved flipping a 2 kg (4.4 lb) weight with the stomach is 1.07 m (3 ft 6 in) by Wang Zhanjun (China) on the set of *Lo Show Dei Record* in Milan, Italy, on 19th April 2009.

丹田弹 2 千克重物的最远距离，是 1.07 米。由中国的王战军于 2009 年 4 月 19 日，在意大利米兰创造。

Fastest time to tear five metal basins in half with the hands
最快速度用手把 5 个金属盆撕成两半

The fastest time to tear five metal basins in half with the hands is one minute 44 seconds and was achieved by Ding Zhaohai (China) on the set of *Zheng Da Zong Yi - Guinness World Records Special* in Beijing, China, on 20th June 2009.

创造最快速度用手把 5 个金属盆撕成两半纪录的，是中国的丁兆海。2009 年 6 月 20 日，丁兆海在北京"正大综艺·吉尼斯中国之夜"节目上，以 1 分 44 秒的速度，用手把 5 个金属盆撕成两半。

Hair cutting - most scissors
单手持最多剪子理发

Wang Zedong (China) styled a head of hair using ten pairs of scissors in one hand, controlling each pair independently, on the set of *Zheng Da Zong Yi - Guinness World Records Special* in Beijing, China, on 31st October 2007.

创造单手持最多剪子理发纪录的，是中国的王泽东。2007 年 10 月 31 日，在"正大综艺 · 吉尼斯中国之夜"节目上，王泽东一只手拿 10 把剪子，且能独立控制每把剪子为人理发。

Highest waterfall diving
最高的瀑布跳水

The highest waterfall dive was 12.19 m (39.99 ft) and was achieved by Di Huanran (China) at the Diaoshuilou Waterfall of Jingbo lake, Mudanjiang City, China, on 5th October 2008.

最高的瀑布跳水纪录，是 12.19 米。由中国的狄焕然于 2008 年 10 月 5 日，在中国牡丹江镜泊湖吊水楼瀑布创造。

Highest bungee jump dive into water
蹦极入水的 最高纪录

The highest bungee jump dive into water is 50 m (164 ft) and was achieved by Zhang Di (China) who jumped from a helicopter in Qindao City, Shandong Province, China, on 15th November 2006.

创造蹦极入水最高纪录的，是中国的张迪。2006 年 11 月 15 日，张迪在中国山东省青岛从悬停在距海面 50 米高的直升机上跳入海中。

Heaviest vehicle pulled by rice bowl suction on the stomach
腹部吸碗拉动的最重汽车

By pressing a rice bowl on his abdominal muscles, Zhang Xingquan (China) was able to create enough suction to pull a 3,305.5 kg (7,287.38 lb) vehicle for 10 meters on the set of *Zheng Da Zong Yi - Guinness World Records Special* in Beijing, China, on 16th December 2006.

　　创造用腹部吸碗拉动最重汽车纪录的，是中国的张兴全。2006 年 12 月 16 日，张兴全在"正大综艺·吉尼斯中国之夜"节目上，用腹部吸碗，将一辆重 3,305.5 千克的汽车拉动 10 米。↑

Heaviest train pulled by rice bowl suction on the stomach
腹部吸碗拉动的最重火车

By pressing a rice bowl on his abdominal muscles, Zhang Xingquan (China) was able to create enough suction to pull a 36.15 tonnes (79,700 lb) train for 40 meters in Dehai City, Jilin Province, China, on 3rd August 2007. The record was attempted for *Zheng Da Zong Yi - Guinness World Records Special* in Beijing, China.

　　创造用腹部吸碗拉动最重火车纪录的，是中国的张兴全。2007 年 8 月 3 日，张兴全在中国吉林省用腹部吸碗，将 36.15 吨重的火车拉动 40 米。

Heaviest vehicle pulled by the eyelids
用眼皮拉动的最重汽车

The heaviest car pulled by the eyelids weighed 1,500 kg (3,307 lb) and was pulled for 10 m (33 ft) by Dong Changsheng (China) through ropes hooked on his lower eyelids in Changchun, China, on 26th September 2006.

创造用眼皮拉动最重汽车纪录的，是中国的董长生。2006 年 9 月 26 日，董长生在中国长春用钩在下眼皮上的绳子，将重 1,500 千克的汽车拉动 10 米。

Heaviest vehicle pulled using earrings
用耳环拉动的最重汽车

The heaviest vehicle pulled using earrings is 1,562 kg (3,443 lb) and was achieved by Gao Lin (China) who attached a car to his earrings by means of a rope and pulled it for 10 m (33 ft) on the set of *Zheng Da Zong Yi - Guinness World Records Special* in Beijing, China, on 19th December 2006.

创造用耳环拉动最重汽车纪录的，是中国的高林。2006 年 12 月 19 日，高林在"正大综艺·吉尼斯中国之夜"节目上，用绳子将一辆 1,562 千克重的汽车拴在自己的耳环上，拉动汽车移动了 10 米。↑

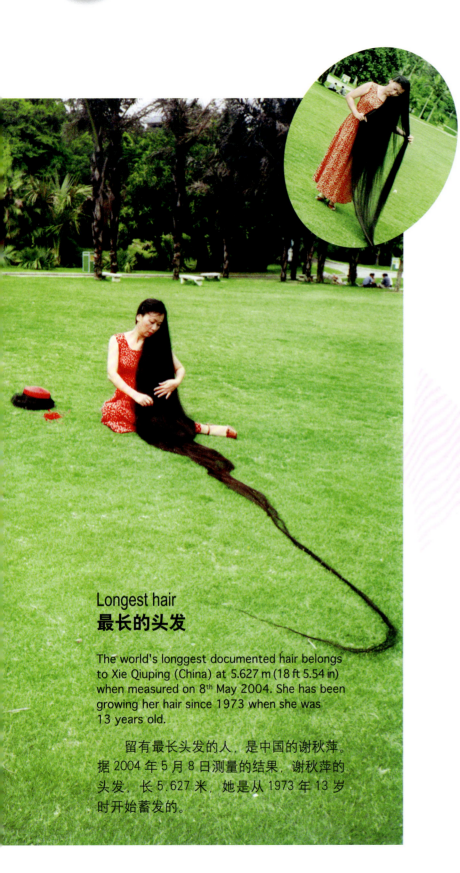

Longest hair
最长的头发

The world's longest documented hair belongs to Xie Qiuping (China) at 5.627 m (18 ft 5.54 in) when measured on 8th May 2004. She has been growing her hair since 1973 when she was 13 years old.

留有最长头发的人，是中国的谢秋萍。据 2004 年 5 月 8 日测量的结果，谢秋萍的头发，长 5.627 米，她是从 1973 年 13 岁时开始蓄发的。

Longest career as a radio presenter/DJ
从事调音师 DJ 职业最长的人

Ray Cordeiro MBE (alias Uncle Ray, b.12th December 1924) has been a regular disc jockey since 1949, first working for the station Rediffusion (Hong Kong) Ltd. and then moving to the now Radio Television Hong Kong on 15th September 1960, where he still has a regular four-hour nightly show called All the Way with Ray transmitted 10 pm - 2 am Monday to Friday.

从事调音师 DJ 职业最长的人，是中国的郭利民（别名 Uncle Ray），生于 1924 年 12 月 12 日。自 1949 年起成为一名职业的电台音乐节目主持人 (DJ)，1960 年 9 月 15 日至今，在中国香港电台每周一至周五晚上 10 点至凌晨 2 点主持一个每晚四小时的节目 —— All the Way with Ray。

Largest hula hoop spun
旋转直径最大的
呼啦圈

The largest hula hoop has a diameter of 5.02 m (16 ft 6 in) and was spun three consecutive times by Bao Runze (China) on the set of *Zheng Da Zong Yi - Guinness World Records Special* in Beijing, China, on 8th November 2008.

　　创造旋转直径最大的呼啦圈纪录的，是中国的包润泽。2008 年 11 月 8 日，包润泽在"正大综艺·吉尼斯中国之夜"节目上，成功旋转直径为 5.02 米的呼啦圈。↑

Largest Indian spun pancake
旋转最大的印度飞饼

The largest Indian spun pancake measured 76 cm (2 ft 5 in) in diametre and was achieved by Cao Huaijiang (China) on the set of *Zheng Da Zong Yi - Guinness World Records Special* in Beijing, China, on 20th June 2009.

　　创造旋转最大的印度飞饼纪录的，是中国的曹怀蒋，他于 2009 年 6 月 20 日，在"正大综艺·吉尼斯中国之夜"节目上成功旋转了直径为 76 厘米的印度飞饼。

Longest continuous ride standing on the seat of a motorcycle
在摩托车座上站立撒把行驶的
最长距离

The longest continuous ride while standing on the seat of a motorcycle and not touching the handlebars is 5.32 km (3.305 miles) by Liu Jichun (China) in Beijing, China, on 13th December 2002.

　　在摩托车座上站立撒把行驶的最长距离，是 5.32 千米。中国的刘继春于 2002 年 12 月 13 日在中国北京创造。

Longest human stomach suction suspension
最长时间人体腹部吸力悬挂

By pressing a rice bowl on his abdominal muscles, Li Kangle (China) was able to create enough suction to suspend himself from a helicopter on a rope for 7 min 6 sec in Pingyi County, Shandong Province, China. The record was attempted for *Zheng Da Zong Yi - Guinness World Records Special* in Beijing, China, on 6th September 2007.

创造最长时间人体腹部吸力悬挂纪录的，是中国的李康乐。2007 年 9 月 6 日，李康乐在"正大综艺·吉尼斯中国之夜"节目外景地——中国山东省平邑县，成功用腹部吸住碗，悬挂于旋转的直升机机身下，在半空中达 7 分 6 秒。

Longest distance riding backwards on a motorcycle
倒骑摩托车的最长距离

The record for the longest backwards motorcycle ride is 150 km (93.21 miles) and was achieved by Hou Xiaobin (China) in Binzhou City, China, on 4th October 2006

倒骑摩托车的最长距离，是 150 千米。由中国的侯晓滨于 2006 年 10 月 4 日，在中国滨州创造。

Most apples snapped in one minute
1 分钟掰断最多的苹果

The most apples snapped in one minute is 33 and was achieved by Ren Chunquan (China) on the set of *Zheng Da Zong Yi - Guinness World Records Special* in Beijing, China, on 10th November 2008.

1 分钟掰断最多苹果的数目，是 33 个。由中国的任春泉于 2008 年 11 月 10 日，在"正大综艺·吉尼斯中国之夜"节目上创造。 ➡

Longest distance on a tightrope with motorcycle (no front wheel)
骑没有前轮的摩托车走钢丝的最长距离

The record for the longest distance covered by a motorcycle (with the front wheel taken off) on a tightrope was 50 m (164 ft), achieved by Chen Shuang Quan (China) in Taiwan, China, on 15th October 2007.

骑没有前轮的摩托车走钢丝的最长距离，是 50 米。由中国的陈双全于 2007 年 10 月 15 日，在台湾创造。

Most banknotes counted by hand (30 seconds)
30 秒手点钞票的最多张数

The greatest number of 100 Chinese Yuan bills counted by hand in 30 seconds is 171 by Song Chao (China), on the set of Zheng Da Zong Yi - Guinness World Records Special in Beijing, China, on 9th November 2008.

30 秒手点钞票的最多张数，是 171 张。由中国的宋超于 2008 年 11 月 9 日，在 "正大综艺·吉尼斯中国之夜" 节目上创造。

Milk squirting from the eye - the fastest time to extinguish five candles
用眼睛喷牛奶灭 5 支蜡烛的最快时间

The fastest time to extinguish five candles by squirting milk from the eye is 17 seconds and was achieved by Ru Anting (China) on the set of Zheng Da Zong Yi - Guinness World Records Special in Beijing, China, on 16th December 2006.

用眼睛喷牛奶灭 5 支蜡烛的最快时间，是 17 秒。由中国的茹安听于 2006 年 12 月 16 日，在 "正大综艺·吉尼斯中国之夜" 节目上创造。

Most 360 spins on a tightrope in two minutes
两分钟内在钢丝上 360 度旋转的最多次数

The most 360 spins on a tightrope in two minutes is 41 and was achieved by Maimaitiaili Abula (China) on the set of *Zheng Da Zong Yi - Guinness World Records Special* in Beijing, China, on 20th September 2007.

两分钟内在钢丝上 360 度旋转的最多次数，是 41 次。由中国的买买提·艾力于 2007 年 9 月 20 日，在"正大综艺·吉尼斯中国之夜"节目上创造。

Most bottles broken in one minute
1 分钟用手掌击碎最多的瓶子

The most bottles broken in one minute is 30 and was achieved by Ling Chunjiang (China) on the set of *Zheng Da Zong Yi - Guinness World Records Special* in Beijing, China, on 31st October 2007.

　　1 分钟用手掌击碎最多瓶子的数目，是 30 个。由中国的凌春江于 2007 年 10 月 31 日，在"正大综艺·吉尼斯中国之夜"节目上创造。←

Most candles extinguished with a pigtail (platted ponytail) in one minute
1 分钟内用辫子打灭最多的蜡烛

The most candles extinguished with a pigtail (platted ponytail) in one minute is eight and was achieved by Chin Chun Yu (China), on the set of *Zheng Da Zong Yi - Guinness World Records Special* in Beijing, China, on 11th November 2008.

　　1 分钟内用辫子打灭最多蜡烛的数目，是 8 根。由中国的钱震宇于 2008 年 11 月 11 日，在"正大综艺·吉尼斯中国之夜"节目上创造。↓

Most cucumbers cut by throwing playing cards in one minute
1 分钟内手掷扑克切断最多黄瓜

The most cucumbers cut by throwing playing cards in one minute is 21 and was achieved by Li Manyuan (China) on the set of *Zheng Da Zong Yi - Guinness World Records Special* in Beijing, China, on 13th November 2008.

　　1 分钟内手掷扑克切断最多黄瓜的数目,是 21 根。由中国的李满员于 2008 年 11 月 13 日,在"正大综艺·吉尼斯中国之夜"节目上创造。↑

The most eggs in cups blown upside down in one minute
1 分钟内吹翻杯子里的鸡蛋最多数目

The most eggs placed in cups blown upside down in one minute is 30 and was achieved by Ding Zhaohai (China) on the set of *Zheng Da Zong Yi - Guinness World Records Special* in Beijing, China, on 31st October 2007.

　　1 分钟内吹翻杯子里的鸡蛋最多数目,是 30 枚。由中国的丁兆海于 2007 年 10 月 31 日,在"正大综艺·吉尼斯中国之夜"节目上创造。→

Memorizing Pi
背诵圆周率位数最多

The record for memorizing Pi was achieved by Lv Chao (China) who recited Pi from memory to 67,890 places, at the Northwest A & F University, Shaanxi Province, China, on 20th November 2005.

　　背诵圆周率位数最多的纪录，由中国的吕超于 2005 年 11 月 20 日创造，共背诵 67,890 位。

Most holes made in a metal barrel with chopsticks in one minute
1 分钟内用筷子在金属桶上扎穿最多的洞

The most holes made in a metal barrel with chopsticks in one minute is 41 and was achieved by Wang Jiao (China) on the set of *Zheng Da Zong Yi - Guinness World Records Special* in Beijing, China, on 30th October 2007.

　　1 分钟内用筷子在金属桶上扎穿最多洞的数目，是 41 个。由中国的王娇于 2007 年 10 月 30 日，在"正大综艺·吉尼斯中国之夜"节目上创造。→

Most chickens spit-roasted simultaneously
同时烧烤最多鸡

The most chickens spit-roasted at one time is 2,008, all of which were stuffed on to a 5 m (16 ft 5 in) high, 20 m (65 ft 7 in) long rotisserie wall and cooked by chef Jiang Bing (China), in Nanning, Guangxi, China, on 24th October 2007.

　创造同时烧烤最多鸡纪录的，是中国的蒋炳。2007 年 10 月 24 日，厨师蒋炳在中国广西省南宁，一人用 5 米高、20 米长的烧烤架，烧烤了 2,008 只鸡。

Most letters typed in alphabetical order with the feet in one minute
1 分钟内用脚按字母排序打出最多的字母

The most letters typed with feet in alphabetical order in one minite is 231 and was achieved by Liu Wei (China) on the set of *Zheng Da Zong Yi - Guinness World Records Special* in Beijing, China, on 18th June 2009.

1 分钟内用脚按字母排序打出最多字母的数目，是 231 个。由中国的刘伟于 2009 年 6 月 18 日，在"正大综艺·吉尼斯中国之夜"节目上创造。→

Most mental calculations in one minute
1 分钟内最多的珠心算

The most mental calculations made in one minute is eight and was achieved by Chen Ranran (China) on the set of *Zheng Da Zong Yi - Guinness World Records Special* in Beijing, China, on 2nd November 2007. Every calculation consisted of 11 numbers for a total of 120 digits. The calculations were supplied in a sealed envelope by the Abacus and Mental Arithmetics Federation.

1 分钟内最多的珠心算，是 8 次。由中国的陈冉冉于 2007 年 11 月 2 日，在"正大综艺·吉尼斯中国之夜"节目上创造。每道珠心算题包括 11 个数字，共 120 位。←

Most needles threaded blindfolded in one minute
1 分钟内蒙眼睛穿针的最多数目

The most needles threaded blindfolded in one minute is 39 and was achieved by Wan Fuquan (China) on the set of *Zheng Da Zong Yi - Guinness World Records Special* in Beijing, China, on 8th November 2008.

1 分钟内蒙眼睛穿针的最多数目，是 39 根。由中国的万福全于 2008 年 11 月 8 日，在"正大综艺·吉尼斯中国之夜"节目上创造。

Most metal basins pierced by throwing chopsticks
1 分钟内投掷筷子穿破最多金属盆的数目

The most metal basins pierced by throwing chopsticks is 32 and was achieved by Yang Zhengqing (China) on the set of *Zheng Da Zong Yi - Guinness World Records Special* in Beijing, China, on 12th November 2008.

1 分钟内投掷筷子穿破最多金属盆的数目，是 32 个。由中国的杨正清于 2008 年 11 月 12 日，在"正大综艺·吉尼斯中国之夜"节目上创造。↓

Most neckties tied with a four-in-hand knot in one minute
1 分钟内打出最多领带结的数目

The most neckties tied with a four-in-hand knot in one minute is 13 and was achieved by Yu Zhenzhen (China) on the set of *Zheng Da Zong Yi - Guinness World Records Special* in Beijing, China, on 14th November 2008.

　　1 分钟内打出最多领带结的数目，是 13 个。由中国的于真真于 2008 年 11 月 14 日，在"正大综艺·吉尼斯中国之夜"节目上创造。←

Most vertical water squirts in one minute
1 分钟内手挤喷射水柱的最多次数

The most vertical water squirts in one minute is 104 and was achieved by Chen Chun (China) on the set of *Zheng Da Zong Yi - Guinness World Records Special* in Beijing, China, on 18th June 2009.

　　1 分钟内手挤喷射水柱的最多次数，是 104 次。由中国的陈椿于 2009 年 6 月 18 日，在"正大综艺·吉尼斯中国之夜"节目上创造。

Most pieces of glass broken by finger flicking in one minute
1 分钟内用手指弹碎玻璃的最多块数

The most pieces of glass broken with flicking one finger in one minute is 32 and was achieved by Zhang Guowu (China) on the set of *Zheng Da Zong Yi - Guinness World Records Special* in Beijing, China, on 28th October 2007.

　　1 分钟内用手指弹碎玻璃的最多块数，是 32 块。由中国的张国武于 2007 年 10 月 28 日，在"正大综艺·吉尼斯中国之夜"节目上创造。→

Most potato stripes cut on a balloon in 30 seconds
30 秒钟内在气球上切出最多土豆丝的数目

The most potato stripes cut on a balloon in 30 seconds is 38 and was achieved by Tan Xingyong (China) on the set of *Zheng Da Zong Yi - Guinness World Records Special* in Beijing, China, on 31st October 2007.

　　30 秒钟内在气球上切出最多土豆丝的数目，是 38 根。由中国的谭兴勇于 2007 年 10 月 31 日，在"正大综艺·吉尼斯中国之夜"节目上创造。 ←

Most spoons twisted in one minute
1 分钟内徒手掰弯最多勺子的数目

The most spoons twisted by 180 degrees in one minute with bare hands is five and was achieved by Kong Tai (China) at the Buffalo, Beijing, China, on 18th December 2006.

　　1 分钟内徒手掰弯最多勺子的数目，是 5 个。由中国的孔太于 2006 年 12 月 18 日，在中国北京 Buffalo 创造。

Most strings of noodle threaded
1 个针眼内穿过最多根的面条

The most strings of noodle threaded using a needle is 39 and was achieved by Li Enhai (China) on the set of *Zheng Da Zong Yi - Guinness World Records Special* in Beijing, China, on 15th December 2006.

　　1 个针眼内穿过最多根面条的数目，是 39 根。由中国的厉恩海于 2006 年 12 月 15 日,在"正大综艺·吉尼斯中国之夜"节目上创造。 →

Most standing jumps on to raw eggs in one minute
1 分钟内从地上跳到生鸡蛋上，但鸡蛋没碎的最多次数

The most standing jumps on to raw eggs without breaking them is six and was achieved by Lan Guangping (China) on the set of *Zheng Da Zong Yi - Guinness World Records Special* in Beijing, China, on 22nd June 2009.

　　1 分钟内从地上跳到生鸡蛋上，但鸡蛋没碎的最多次数，是 6 次。由中国的兰广平于 2009 年 6 月 22 日，在"正大综艺·吉尼斯中国之夜"节目上创造。

Most walnuts crushed by the hand in one minute
1 分钟内用手砸碎核桃最多的数目

The most walnuts crushed by the hand in one minute is 51 and was achieved by Wei Lide (China) on the set of *Zheng Da Zong Yi - Guinness World Records Special* in Beijing, China, on 18th September 2007.

　　1 分钟内用手砸碎核桃最多的数目，是 51 个。由中国的魏立德于 2007 年 9 月 18 日，在"正大综艺·吉尼斯中国之夜"节目上创造。→

Motorcycle moving ramp jump mid air crossing furthest distance
摩托车对飞跨越移动坡道的最长距离

The record for the biggest gap covered by motorcycle moving ramp jump mid air parallel crossing is 16 m (52 ft 5 in) and was achieved by Sun Zhaohui and Han Baohua (both China) in Shenzhen City, China, on 5th November 2008.

　　摩托车对飞跨越移动坡道的最长距离，是 16 米。由中国的孙兆辉和韩宝华于 2008 年 11 月 5 日，在中国深圳创造。

Shortest man - living
在世的最矮的
成年男人

The shortest living man is Lin Yih-Chih (Taiwan, China) at 67.5 cm (27 in). He is confined to a wheelchair because of osteogenesis imperfecta.

目前在世的最矮的成年男人，是台湾的林煜智，高 67.5 厘米。他因骨生成缺陷只能坐轮椅生活。

Smallest distance parallel parking
最小距离汽车漂移入位

Sun Jinguo (China) from Zhengzhi Car Stunts Performance Team parked a Chery QQ automobile in a space that was only 32 cm (12.6 in) longer than the car, in Wuhu City, China, on 14th June 2009.

成功实现最小距离汽车漂移入位的纪录，即前后两车的车距只比驾驶入位的车身长 32 厘米。由中国的孙金国于 2009 年 6 月 14 日，在中国芜湖驾驶奇瑞 QQ 汽车创造。

Steepest gradient - tightrope walking
最陡的钢丝行走

Abulaiti Maijun (China) completed a 58.24 m (191 ft 0.9 in) tightrope walk, with an average slope of 34.15 degrees in Xinjiang, China, on 24th August 2007. The record was attempted for *Zheng Da Zong Yi - Guinness World Records Special* in Beijing, China.

最陡的钢丝行走纪录，由中国的阿布来提·麦均于 2007 年 8 月 24 日，在中国新疆创造。坡度为 34.15 度，行走了 58.24 米。

Sports and Games

体育与游戏

体育与游戏
Sports and Games

Fastest 20 cone slalom on inline skates
单排轮滑过桩的最快时间

The fastest 20 cone slalom on inline skates is 5.04 seconds and was achieved by Guo Fang (China) on the set of *Zheng Da Zong Yi - Guinness World Records Special* in Beijing, China, on 14th November 2008.

单排轮滑过桩的最快时间，是5.04秒。由中国的郭方于2008年11月14日，在"正大综艺·吉尼斯中国之夜"节目上创造。↓

Fastest road relay (female)
道路接力赛的最快纪录（女子）

2:11.41, People's Republic of China (Jiang Bo, Dong Yanmei, Zhao Fengdi, Ma Zaijie, Lan Lixin, Li Na) Beijing, China, 28th February 1998.

女子道路接力赛的最快纪录，是2分11秒41。由中国的姜波、董艳梅、赵凤婷、马再捷、兰丽新、林娜于1998年2月28日，在中国北京创造。

Fastest 15 m speed climb (female)
15 米攀岩比赛的最快速度（女子）

The fastest International Federation of Sport Climbing 15 m climb by a woman is 10.58 seconds by Li Chunhua (China) in Qinghai, China, on 27th June 2008.

女子15米攀岩比赛的最快速度，是10.58秒。由中国的李春华于2008年6月27日，在中国青海省创造。

Fastest swim long course 200 m butterfly (female)
200 米蝶泳的最快纪录（女子）

2:04.18, Liu Zige (China) The Water Cube, Beijing, China, on 14th August 2008.

女子200米蝶泳的最快纪录，是2分4秒18。由中国的刘子歌于2008年8月14日，在中国北京的水立方创造。

Fastest time to solve a Rubik's Cube - blindfolded
蒙眼复原魔方的最快时间

The record for the fastest solve of a Rubik's cube while blindfolded is 41.16 seconds and was set by Chen Danyang (China) on the set of *Zheng Da Zong Yi - Guinness World Records Special* in Beijing, China, on 28th October 2007.

　　蒙眼复原魔方的最快时间，是 41.16 秒。由中国的陈丹阳于 2007 年 10 月 28 日，在"正大综艺·吉尼斯中国之夜"节目上创造。←

Fastest tightrope walk over 100 m
100 米钢丝行走的最快速度

The fastest tightrope walk over 100 m is 44.63 seconds and was achieved by Aisikaier Wubulikasimu (China) at Taimu Mountain Scenic Spot, Fuding City, Fujian Province, China, on 27th October 2009.

　　100 米钢丝行走的最快速度，是 44.63 秒。由中国的艾斯开尔·乌布力喀斯木于 2009 年 10 月 27 日，在中国福建省福鼎太姥山风景区创造。

Furthest distance walking on stilts in 24 hours
24 小时踩高跷行走的最远距离

Saimaiti Yiming (China) completed a distance of 79.6 km (49.4 miles) in 24 hours walking on stilts around Shanshan County, Xinjiang, China, from 30th September to 1st October 2003. His stilts measured 73 cm (28.7 in) from the ground to his ankle and weighed 10 kg (22 lb).

　　24 小时踩高跷行走的最远距离，是 79.6 千米。由中国的赛买提·依明于 2003 年 9 月 30 日至 10 月 1 日，在中国新疆鄯善县周边完成。其高跷从地面至脚踝有 73 厘米，重 10 千克。

Fastest marathon running backwards (male)
倒跑马拉松的最快纪录（男子）

Xu Zhenjun (China) ran the fastest backwards marathon by completing the Beijing International Marathon, China, in a time of 3 hr 43 min 39 sec on 17th October 2004.

男子倒跑马拉松的最快纪录，是 3 小时 43 分 39 秒。由中国的许振军于 2004 年 10 月 17 日，在中国北京国际马拉松比赛中创造。↑

Fastest time-International Dragon Boat Races
国际龙舟赛的最快时间

Instituted in 1975 and held annually in Hong Kong, China, the fastest time achieved for the 640 m (2,099 ft/700 yd) course is 2 min 27.45 sec by the Chinese Shun De team on 30th June 1985.

国际龙舟赛的最快时间，是以 2 分 27.45 秒的速度完成 640 米的赛程。这个纪录由中国的顺德队于 1985 年 6 月 30 日，在中国香港举办的国际龙舟赛上创造。

Fastest run 3,000 m (female)
3,000 米赛跑的最快纪录（女子）

8:06.11, Wang Junxia (China) Beijing, China, 13th September 1993.

女子 3,000 米赛跑的最快纪录，是 8 分 6 秒 11。由中国的王军霞于 1993 年 9 月 13 日，在中国北京创造。 →

Fastest 15 m speed climb (male)
15 米攀岩比赛的最快速度（男子）

The fastest International Federation of Sport Climbing 15 m climb by a man is 7.35 seconds by Zhong Qixin (China) in Qinghai, China, on 27th June 2008.

男子 15 米攀岩比赛的最快速度，是 7.35 秒。由中国的钟齐鑫于 2008 年 6 月 27 日，在中国青海省创造。

Fastest time to ascend a sand dune
骑摩托车攀登沙山的最快时间

The fastest time to ascend a sand dune (418 m, 1371 ft) on a motorcycle is 6 minutes 2 seconds, achieved by Tao Yongming (China) for *Zheng Da Zong Yi - Guinness World Records Special* when he drove his motorcycle to the top of Bilutu Peak in Badanjilin desert, Inner Mongolia Autonomous Region, China, on 23rd September 2009.

骑摩托车攀登沙山（418 米高）的最快时间，是 6 分 2 秒。由中国的陶永明于 2009 年 9 月 23 日，在中国内蒙古巴丹吉林沙漠必鲁图峰创造。 ↓

Fastest run 1,500 m (female)
1,500 米赛跑的最快纪录（女子）

3:50.46, Qu Yunxia (China), Beijing, China, 11th September 1993.

女子 1,500 米赛跑的最快纪录，是 3 分 50 秒 46。由中国的曲云霞于 1993 年 9 月 11 日，在中国北京创造。

Fastest 31-legged race (50 m)
31 足跑的最快速度（50 米）

The fastest 31-legged race (50 m) was 8.41 seconds and was achieved by the students from Shao Lin Tagou Martial Arts School in Dengfeng City, Henan Province, China, on 12th May 2009.

50 米 31 足跑的最快速度，是 8.41 秒。由中国河南省登封少林寺塔沟武术学校于 2009 年 5 月 12 日创造。

137

Highest jump on spring loaded stilts
踩弹簧高跷跳高的最高高度

The highest jump on spring loaded stilts is 2.71 m (8.89 ft) and was achieved by Wu Jialong in Dengfeng City, Henan province, China, on 17th September 2008.

踩弹簧高跷跳高的最高高度，是 2.71 米。由中国的吴家龙于 2008 年 9 月 17 日，在中国河南省登封创造。→

Highest walls climbed with feet only in 30 seconds
30 秒内双脚蹬墙爬的最高高度

The highest wall climbed with feet only in 30 seconds is 13.3 m (43 ft 7.6 in) and was achieved by Gao Guixian (China) from Shao Lin Tagou Martial Arts School in Dengfeng City, Henan Province, China, on 12th November 2009.

30 秒内双脚蹬墙爬的最高高度，是 13.3 米。由中国少林塔沟武术学校的高贵贤于 2009 年 11 月 12 日，在中国河南省登封创造。

Highest ramp jump on inline skates
最高的轮滑鞋平台跳跃

The highest ramp jump on inline skates is 4.7 m (15 ft 5.04 in) and was achieved by Zhang baoxiang (China) for *Zheng Da Zong Yi - Guinness World Records Special* in Beijing, China, on 5th November 2009.

最高的轮滑鞋平台跳跃纪录，是 4.7 米。由中国的张宝祥于 2009 年 11 月 5 日，在中国北京创造。

Highest annual betting turnover for a racing club
一年内下注金额最多的赛马俱乐部

The total betting turnover of the Hong Kong Jockey Club for the 1997/98 season was $12.1 billion (£7.3 billion). Approximately one third of Hong Kong's adult population bets on horse racing during the season. Bets can be placed at the racecourse, or at 120 sanctioned betting stations throughout Hong Kong.

一年内下注金额最多的赛马俱乐部，是中国香港赛马会。1997 ～ 1998 年度全部下注金额为 121 亿美元，大约有三分之一的香港成年人在这一年度参与。

Highest jump through a hoop
钻圈跳跃的最高高度

The highest jump through a hoop was 3.12 m (10 ft 2 in) and was achieved by Qiu Jiangming (China) of the China National Acrobatic Troupe on the set of *Zheng Da Zong Yi - Guinness World Records Special* in Beijing, China, on 17th June 2009.

钻圈跳跃的最高高度，是 3.12 米。由中国杂技团的邱江明 于 2009 年 6 月 17 日，在"正大 综艺·吉尼斯中国之夜"节目上 创造。→

Heaviest weightlifting 53 kg clean & jerk (female)
53 千克级挺举纪录（女子）

129 kg, Li Ping (China) in Taian City, China, 22nd April 2007.

女子 53 千克级挺举纪录，是 129 千克。由中国的李萍于 2007 年 4 月 22 日，在中国泰安创造。

Heaviest weightlifting 58 kg clean & jerk (female)
58 千克级挺举纪录（女子）

141 kg, Qiu Hongmei (China) in Taian City, China, 23ʳᵈ April 2007.

女子 58 千克级挺举纪录，是 141 千克。由中国的邱红梅于 2007 年 4 月 23 日，在中国泰安创造。

Heaviest weightlifting 48 kg clean & jerk (female)
48 千克级挺举纪录（女子）

120 kg, Chen Xiexia (China) in Taian City, China, 21ˢᵗ April 2007.

女子 48 千克级挺举纪录，是 120 千克。由中国的陈燮霞于 2007 年 4 月 21 日，在中国泰安创造。

Largest martial arts display
最大规模的武术表演

The largest martial arts display was achieved by 33,996 participants in an event organized by Beijing Municipal Bureau of Sports in Beijing, China, on 8ᵗʰ August 2009.

最大规模的武术表演，是 2009 年 8 月 8 日，由中国的北京市体育局组织，在中国北京举行的武术表演，有 33,996 人参加表演。↓

Heaviest weightlifting 69 kg clean & jerk (female)
69 千克级挺举纪录（女子）

158 kg, Liu Chunhong (China) in Beijing, China, 13ʳᵈ August 2008.

女子 69 千克级挺举纪录，是 158 千克。由中国的刘春红于 2008 年 8 月 13 日，在中国北京创造。

Heaviest weightlifting 69 kg clean & jerk (male)
69 千克级挺举纪录（男子）

197 kg, Zhang Guozheng (China) in Qinhuangdao, China, 11th September 2003.

男子 69 千克级挺举纪录，是 197 千克。由中国的张国政于 2003 年 9 月 11 日，在中国秦皇岛创造。

Longest duration balancing on four fingers
用四根手指保持平衡的最长时间

The longest duration balancing on four fingers is 19.23 seconds and was achieved by Wang Weibao (China) on the set of *Zheng Da Zong Yi - Guinness World Records Special* in Beijing, China, on 9th November 2008.

用四根手指保持平衡的最长时间，是 19.23 秒。由中国的王巍堡于 2008 年 11 月 9 日，在"正大综艺·吉尼斯中国之夜"节目上创造。➡

Largest archery tournament
最大规模的射箭比赛

The largest archery tournament was achieved by 332 participants in Xinbaerhuyou Banner, Inner Mongolia Autonomous Region, China, on 22nd August 2009. The event was organized by the Archery Association of Xinbaerhuyou Banner.

最大规模的射箭比赛，于 2009 年 8 月 22 日，在中国内蒙古呼伦贝尔新巴尔虎右旗举行，有 332 人参加。➡

141

Longest time on a balance board holding a glass on the forehead
前额顶盛满葡萄酒的玻璃杯在平衡板上站立的最长时间

The longest time on a balance board holding a full glass of wine on the forehead is one hour and eight minutes and was achieved by Tang Guoai (China) on the set of *Zheng Da Zong Yi - Guinness World Records Special* in Beijing, China, on 19th December 2006.

前额顶盛满葡萄酒的玻璃杯在平衡板上站立的最长时间，是 1 小时 8 分钟。由中国的唐国爱于 2006 年 12 月 19 日，在"正大综艺·吉尼斯中国之夜"节目上创造。↓

Longest marathon playing Mahjong
耗时最长的麻将马拉松

Zheng Taishun, Xie Lili, Chen Zhujun and Lin Shouzhun (all China) played Mahjong from 12:00 a.m. noon on 18th March 2007 to 5:58 p.m. on 19th March 2007, for a total of 29 hours and 58 minutes, in Taishun Board Game & Playing Cards Club, Fuzhou City, Fujian Province, China.

耗时最长的麻将马拉松，是中国的郑太顺等四人在中国福建省创造的，他们于 2007 年 3 月 18 日中午 12 点开始打麻将，至 3 月 19 日下午 5 点 58 分结束，总计耗时 29 小时 58 分。

Loudest scream by a crowd (indoors)
集体发出的最响的尖叫声（室内）

The loudest scream by a crowd (indoors) is 131.6 dba and was achieved by the audience of FAMA's concert at Hong Kong International Trade & Exhibition Centre in Hong Kong, China, on 6th September 2009. The event was organized by PrimeCredit Limited.

集体在室内发出的最响的尖叫声，是131.6分贝。该纪录由"农夫音乐会"的观众于2009年9月6日，在中国香港国际贸易展览中心创造。→

Longest shuttlecock control with feet
用脚连续踢毽的最长时间

Li Huifeng (China) juggled a shuttlecock for 4 hr 40 min non-stop using only her feet, without the shuttlecock ever touching the ground on the set of *Zheng Da Zong Yi - Guinness World Records Special* in Beijing, China, on 21st December 2006.

用脚连续踢毽的最长时间，是4小时40分。由中国的李汇凤于2006年12月21日，在"正大综艺·吉尼斯中国之夜"节目上创造。←

Furthest pool rescue marathon
最远距离的马拉松泳池救援

The furthest pool rescue distance is 19,300 m (63,320 ft) and was completed by the Wong Tai Sin District Life Saving Society at Morse Park Swimming Pool, Kowloon, Hong Kong, China, on 31st August 2002.

最远距离的马拉松泳池救援纪录，是19.3千米。由中国的黄大仙区救生协会于2002年8月31日，在中国香港九龙的摩士公园游泳池创造。

Largest Mahjong tournament
最大规模的麻将大赛

The largest Mahjong tournament is the First Super Cup Mahjong Tournament held by Gi Tiene International Co., Ltd. (Taiwan, China) between 8th December 2007 and 3rd February 2008. The competition featured 14,886 individual players from all over Taiwan, China.

最大规模的麻将大赛，是 2007 年 12 月 8 日至 2008 年 2 月 3 日，由台湾"超级杯"娱乐有限公司举办的第一届超级杯麻将大赛，全台湾共有 14,886 名选手参赛。

Largest Wing Chun display
最大规模的咏春拳表演

The largest Wing Chun display was achieved by 754 participants at an event organized by World Wing Chun Union and Hong Kong Wing Chun Union in Hong Kong, China, on 7th November 2009.

最大规模的咏春拳表演，由世界咏春拳协会和中国香港咏春拳协会组织，于 2009 年 11 月 7 日，在中国香港举行，共有 754 人参加表演。↓

Largest Mongolian wrestling tournament
最大规模的蒙古式摔跤比赛

The largest Mongolian wrestling tournament was held in Bayanwula, West Ujimqin Banner, Inner Mongolia, China, between 28th July and 1st August 2004 and featured 2,048 competitors.

最大规模的蒙古式摔跤比赛，于 2004 年 7 月 28 日至 8 月 1 日，在中国内蒙古西乌珠穆沁旗巴彦乌拉镇举行，共有 2,048 名选手参赛。↑

Largest golf tournament underwater
最大规模的水下高尔夫比赛

The largest underwater golf tournament had five players, all competing following regular golf rules in a 15 m (50 ft) deep water tank at Zuohai Aquarium in Fuzhou city, Fujian province, China, on 28th May 2007.

最大规模的水下高尔夫比赛，于 2007 年 5 月 28 日，在中国福州左海海底世界举办。共有 5 支参赛队伍，在水下 15 米深的隧道里按正常高尔夫球赛规则进行比赛。

Largest parade of bicycles
最大规模的自行车游行

The largest parade of bicycles consisted of 2,284 bicycles and was organized by Sports Affairs Council, Taichung County Government, Da Jia Jenn Lann Temple, and Volvic Taiwan in Taichung, Taiwan, China, on 21st February 2009.

最大规模的自行车游行，于 2009 年 2 月 21 日，在台湾台中举行，共有 2,284 辆自行车参加。

Largest one day golf tournament
一日内参赛人员最多的高尔夫比赛

The largest one day golf tournament consisted of 1,019 participants and was achieved by Golfers 512 Fund Raising Campaign (China) at Mission Hills Golf Club in Shenzhen, China, on 12th June 2009.

一日内参赛人员最多的高尔夫比赛，是 2009 年 6 月 12 日在中国深圳观澜湖高尔夫球场举办的"高球界 5·12 关爱行动 2009"慈善高尔夫球赛，共有 1,019 人参赛。↑

Most fish caught in one net using traditional winter fishing techniques
单网传统冰下捕鱼量最高

The most fish caught in one single net using traditional fishing techniques is 168,000 kg (370,376.6 lb), when 135 fishermen used horsepower to drag the fishing net from the frozen Chagan Lake during in an event organized by the Chagan Lake Fishery of Qian Gorlosi Mongolian Autonomous County, Jilin Province, China, on 3rd January 2009.

单网传统冰下捕鱼量的最高纪录，是 168,000 千克。2009 年 1 月 3 日，由中国吉林省前郭尔罗斯蒙古族自治县查干湖渔场组织，135 个渔民从结了冰的查干湖中用马力拖出渔网。

Most official Olympic mascots
一届奥运会中最多的吉祥物

In November 2005, the Beijing Organizing Committee for the Games of the XXIX Olympiad (BOCOG) introduced their five official mascots for the 2008 Games - the highest number since the competition began. These five Fuwa, as they were known, are cartoon depictions of a carp (Beibei), a panda (Jingjing), the Olympic flame (Huanhuan), a Tibetan antelope (Yingying) and a swallow (Nini), which symbolise the sea, forests, fire, earth and air, and whose names, when put together in Chinese, read "Bejing Welcomes You!"

2008 年第 29 届北京奥运会有 5 个吉祥物 (福娃)，是奥林匹克竞赛以来数目最多的。5 个 "福娃" 分别象征鱼（贝贝）、大熊猫（晶晶）、奥林匹克圣火（欢欢）、藏羚羊（迎迎）和燕子（妮妮），它们代表了海洋、森林、火、大地和天空。它们的名字连在一起是 "北京欢迎你"。↓

Most participants in a swimming relay in one hour
1 小时内游泳接力最多参与人数

The most participants in a swimming relay in one hour is 254 in an event organized by the Hong Kong Blind Sports Association in Hong Kong, China, on 19th October 2008.

1 小时内游泳接力最多参与人数，是 254 人。该纪录是在 2008 年 10 月 19 日，由中国香港盲人体育会组织的"1 小时游泳接力活动"时创造。

Most forward walkovers in one hour
1 小时内前滚翻的最多次数

The record for the most forward walkovers in one hour is 1,015 and was set by Chung Kwun Ying (Hong Kong) at Sha Tin Racecourse, Hong Kong, China, on 4th November, 2001.

1 小时内前滚翻的最多次数，是 1,015 个。由中国的钟冠英于 2001 年 11 月 4 日，在中国香港沙田马场创造。

Most forward flips in a minute
1 分钟前头翻的最多次数

The most forward flips in a minute is 65 and was achieved by Li Jingguan (China) at the Shao Lin Tagou Martial Arts School on 22nd November 2006.

1 分钟前头翻的最多次数，是 65 个。由中国的李警官于 2006 年 11 月 22 日，在中国河南省少林塔沟武术学校创造。

Most people jumping on spring loaded stilts
踩弹簧高跷跳跃的最多人数

The most people jumping on spring loaded stilts is 103 and was achieved by Shao Lin Tagou Martial Arts School in Dengfeng City, Henan Province, China, on 17th September 2008.

踩弹簧高跷跳跃的最多人数，是 103 人。由中国河南省登封少林塔沟武术学校于 2008 年 9 月 17 日创造。↓

Most people controlling volleyballs
同时垫排球的最多人数

The record for the most people controlling volleyballs is 299 and was achieved by the people of Taiwan at YungShin Sports Park, in Taichung County, Taiwan, China, on 2nd October 2008.

同时垫排球的最多人数，是 299 人。2008 年 10 月 2 日在台湾台中创造。

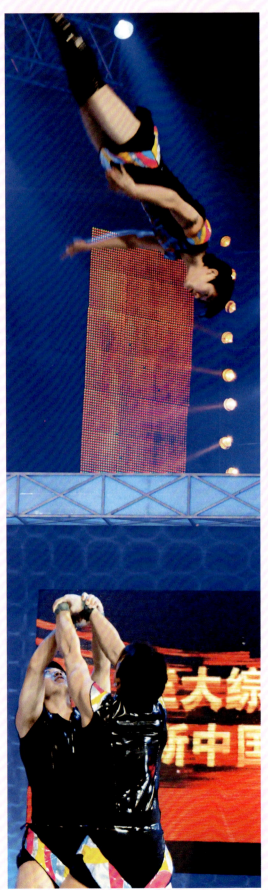

Most consecutive flips on hands held by two people
在两人手上连续空翻的最多次数

The most consecutive flips on hands held by two people is 19 and was achieved by Zang Shibo, Jiang Tongbao and Gao Xuefeng (All China) on the set of *Zheng Da Zong Yi - Guinness World Records Special* in Beijing, China, on 14th November 2008.

在两人手上连续空翻的最多次数，是 19 次。由中国的臧世博、姜佟宝、高学峰于 2008 年 11 月 14 日，在"正大综艺·吉尼斯中国之夜"节目上创造。←↓

Most backwards flips in one minute with head
1 分钟后头翻的最多次数

The most backwards flips in one minute is 46 and was achieved by Liu Hecong (China) at the Shao Lin Tagou Martial Arts School in Dengfeng, Henan Province, China, on 22nd November 2006.

1 分钟后头翻的最多次数，是 46 次。由中国的刘合聪于 2006 年 11 月 22 日，在中国河南省登封少林塔沟武术学校创造。

Most consecutive foot juggling flips
连续蹬人空翻的最多次数

The record for the most consecutive foot juggling flips is 90 and was achieved by Hou Yanan and Jiang Tiantian (both China) from the Wuqiao County Aerobatic Group on the set of *Zheng Da Zong Yi - Guinness World Records Special* in Beijing, China, on 19th September 2007.

连续蹬人空翻的最多次数，是 90 次。由中国吴桥杂技团的侯亚楠和姜甜甜于 2007 年 9 月 19 日，在"正大综艺·吉尼斯中国之夜"节目上创造。→

Most diabolo juggling catches on the back in one minute
1 分钟背后抛接三个空竹的最多次数

The most diabolo juggling catches on the back in one minute is 67 and was achieved by Chen Yun (China) on the set of *Zheng Da Zong Yi - Guinness World Records Special* in Beijing, China, on 12th November 2008.

1 分钟背后抛接三个空竹的最多次数，是 67 次。由中国的陈云于 2008 年 11 月 12 日，在"正大综艺·吉尼斯中国之夜"节目上创造。→

Most hula hoops caught and spun in one minute
1 分钟内接住并旋转呼啦圈的最多次数

The most hula hoops caught and spun in one minute is 236 and was achieved by Liu Rongrong (China) on the set of *Zheng Da Zong Yi - Guinness World Records Special* in Beijing, China, on 17th September 2007.

1 分钟内接住并旋转呼啦圈的最多次数，是 236 次。由中国的刘荣荣于 2007 年 9 月 17 日，在"正大综艺·吉尼斯中国之夜"节目上创造。→

Most open umbrellas balanced simultaneously
同时蹬最多的打开的伞

The most open umbrellas balanced simultaneously is eight and was achieved by Liu Lina (China) on the set of *Zheng Da Zong Yi - Guinness World Records Special* in Beijing, China, on 21st June 2009.

　　同时蹬最多的打开的伞，是 8 把。由中国的刘丽娜于 2009 年 6 月 21 日，在"正大综艺·吉尼斯中国之夜"节目上创造。→

Most stacked chairs balanced on
在最多层叠起的椅子上保持平衡

The record for balancing on the most stacked chairs is 11 and was achieved by Luo Jun from the Zun Yi Acrobatic Group (China) on the set of *Zheng Da Zong Yi - Guinness World Records Special* in Beijing, China, on 15th September 2007.

　　在最多层叠起的椅子上保持平衡纪录的，是来自中国遵义杂技团的罗军。2007 年 9 月 15 日，在"正大综艺·吉尼斯中国之夜"节目上，罗军成功地在 11 把叠起的椅子上保持了平衡。

Most stacked benches held between the teeth
用牙齿顶起最多的长凳

The most benches held between the teeth is 14 and was achieved by Guo Guozhi (China) on the set of *Zheng Da Zong Yi - Guinness World Records Special* in Beijing, China, on 19th December 2006.

　　用牙齿顶起最多的长凳，是 14 个。由中国的郭国直于 2006 年 12 月 19 日，在"正大综艺·吉尼斯中国之夜"节目上创造。

Most pirouettes on pointe on the head
在头顶上做芭蕾脚尖旋转的最多次数

The most pirouettes on pointe on the head is three and was achieved by Wu Zhengdan (China), who balanced on the head of her husband, Wei Baohua (China), and performed three classical pirouettes on the set of *Zheng Da Zong Yi - Guinness World Records Special* in Beijing, China, on 21st December 2006.

在头顶上做最多的芭蕾脚尖旋转的最多次数，是 3 次。2006 年 12 月 21 日，在"正大综艺·吉尼斯中国之夜"节目上，中国的吴正丹在其丈夫魏葆华的头顶上做了 3 个芭蕾脚尖旋转。←

Most one finger push ups in 30 seconds
30 秒单指做俯卧撑的最多次数

The most one finger push ups in 30 seconds is 12 and was achieved by Fu Bingli (China) on the set of *Zheng Da Zong Yi - Guinness World Records Special* in Beijing, China, on 21st June 2009.

30 秒单指做俯卧撑的最多次数，是 12 次。由中国的傅丙利于 2009 年 6 月 21 日，在"正大综艺·吉尼斯中国之夜"节目上创造。↓

153

Most sheets of glass pierced with needles in one minute
1 分钟内用针刺穿玻璃的最多数目

The most sheets of glass pierced with needles in one minute is 21 and was achieved Jiang Zhan (China) on the set of *Zheng Da Zong Yi - Guinness World Records Special* in Beijing, China, on 15th December 2006.

　　1 分钟内用针刺穿玻璃的最多数目，是 21 块。由中国的蒋战于 2006 年 12 月 15 日，在"正大综艺·吉尼斯中国之夜"节目上创造。↓ →

Most times to flash two ping pong balls with the mouth
用嘴连续抛接 2 只乒乓球的最多次数

The most times to flash two ping pong balls with the mouth is 180 and was achieved by Jiang Guoying (China) on the set of *Zheng Da Zong Yi - Guinness World Records Special* in Beijing, China, on 22nd June 2009.

用嘴连续抛接 2 只乒乓球的最多次数，是 180 次。由中国的姜国营于 2009 年 6 月 22 日，在"正大综艺·吉尼斯中国之夜"节目上创造。←

Most skips with an iron chain while sitting in 30 seconds
30 秒内坐姿用铁链跳绳的最多次数

The most skips with an iron chain in a sitting position in 30 seconds is 104 and was achieved by Liu Ningbo (China) on the set of *Zheng Da Zong Yi - Guinness World Records Special* in Beijing, China, on 1st November 2007.

30 秒内坐姿用铁链跳绳的最多次数，是 104 次。由中国的刘宁波于 2007 年 11 月 1 日，在"正大综艺·吉尼斯中国之夜"节目上创造。↓

Most bowls broken with one finger in one minute
1 分钟内用单指打破碗的最多数目

The most bowls broken with one finger in one minute is 102 and was achieved by Fan Weipeng (China) on the set of *Lo Show Dei Record*, in Milan, Italy, on 11th April 2009.

1 分钟内用单指打破碗的最多数目，是 102 个。由中国的樊伟鹏于 2009 年 4 月 11 日，在意大利米兰创造。

Most body revolutions with head and feet on the ground in one minute
1 分钟内头脚着地旋转身体的最多次数

The most body revolutions with head and feet on the ground is 51 and was achieved by Zhang Disheng (China) in Fengtai Sports Center in Beijing, China, on 19th June 2009.

1 分钟内头脚着地旋转身体的最多次数，是 51 次。由中国的张迪升于 2009 年 6 月 19 日，在中国北京丰台体育馆创造。

Most pig iron bars broken with the head in one minute
1 分钟内用头砸断生铁条的最多数目

The most pig iron bars broken with the head in one minute is 29 and was achieved by Wang Xianfa (China) on the set of *Lo Show Dei Record*, in Milan, Italy, on 25th April 2009.

1 分钟内用头砸断生铁条的最多数目，是 29 根。由中国的王宪法于 2009 年 4 月 25 日，在意大利米兰创造。

Most wins of the Sudirman Cup
苏迪曼杯夺冠的最多次数

The most wins at the mixed World Team Badminton Championships for the Sudirman Cup (instituted in 1989) is seven by China in 1995, 1997, 1999, 2001, 2005, 2007 and 2009.

苏迪曼杯夺冠次数最多的国家，是中国。七次夺冠，分别在 1995 年、1997 年、1999 年、2001 年、2005 年、2007 年和 2009 年。

Most backward flips on spring loaded stilts
踩弹簧高跷后空翻的最多次数

The most consecutive backward flips on spring loaded stilts is 25 and was achieved by Yuan Shiwei in Dengfeng city, Henan Province, China, on 17th September 2008.

踩弹簧高跷后空翻的最多次数，是 25 次。由中国的袁世伟于 2008 年 9 月 17 日，在中国河南省登封创造。

Most diabolo catches in one minute
1分钟内抛接空竹的最多次数

Wang Yueqiu (China) threw and caught a diabolo a minimum of 6 m (19 ft 8 in) high a total of 16 times in one minute on the set of *Zheng Da Zong Yi - Guinness World Records Special* in Beijing, China, on 20th September 2007.

1分钟内抛接空竹的最多次数，是16次，每次至少6米高。由中国的王跃秋于2007年9月20日，在"正大综艺·吉尼斯中国之夜"节目上创造。 →

Most consecutive football passes
足球连续传球的最多次数

The most consecutive football passes is 557 and was set by members of the McDonald's Youth Football Scheme, Tsing Yi, Hong Kong, China, on 4th May 2002.

足球连续传球的最多次数，是557次。由中国香港麦当劳青年训练营的成员于2002年5月4日，在中国香港创造。

157

Most horizontal bar backwards spins in one minute
1分钟内做单杠后旋转的最多次数

The most horizontal bar backwards spins in one minute is 63 and was achieved by Wang Jue (China) on the set of *Zheng Da Zong Yi - Guinness World Records Special* in Beijing, China, on 21st June 2009.

1分钟内做单杠后旋转的最多次数，是63次。由中国的王决于2009年6月21日，在"正大综艺·吉尼斯中国之夜"节目上创造。

Most football touches with the head in one minute (male)
1 分钟内用头颠足球的最多次数（男子）

The most touches of a football in one minute, using only the head, while keeping the ball in the air, is 341 by Gao Chong (China) on the set of *Zheng Da Zong Yi - Guinness World Records Special* in Beijing, China, on 3rd November 2007.

　　1 分钟内用头颠足球的最多次数（男子），是 341 次。由中国的高冲于 2007 年 11 月 3 日，在"正大综艺·吉尼斯中国之夜"节目上创造。↑

Most revolutions hula hooping in one minute
1 分钟转呼拉圈的最多圈数

The record for the most revolutions of a hula hoop in one minute is 211 and was achieved by Xia Tao (China) on the set of *Zheng Da Zong Yi - Guinness World Records Special* in Beijing, China, on 8th November 2008.

　　1 分钟转呼拉圈的最多圈数，是 211 圈。由中国的夏涛于 2008 年 11 月 8 日，在"正大综艺·吉尼斯中国之夜"节目上创造。

Most people playing mahjong simultaneously
同时打麻将的最多人数

The most people playing Mahjong simultaneously was achieved by 492 participants at the Hong Kong International Trade & Exhibition Centre Rotunda Hall 2 in Hong Kong, China, on 20th July 2008.

　　同时打麻将的最多人数，是 492 人。该纪录是 2008 年 7 月 20 日，在中国香港国际会议展览中心创造。

Most wooden sticks broken with spring loaded stilts in one minute
1 分钟内用弹簧高跷劈断木棍的最多数目

The most wooden sticks broken with stilts is 25 and was achieved by Zhu Dianbin (China) on the set of *Zheng Da Zong Yi - Guinness World Records Special* in Beijing, China, on 22nd June 2009.

　　1 分钟内用弹簧高跷劈断木棍的最多数目，是 25 根。由中国的朱殿宾于 2009 年 6 月 22 日，在"正大综艺·吉尼斯中国之夜"节目上创造。

Most kites flown simultaneously by one person
单人同时放飞风筝的最多数目

The record for the most kites flown by one person simultaneously is 43 and was achieved by Ma Qinghua (China) in Weifang City, Shandong Province, China, on 7th November 2006.

　　单人同时放飞风筝的最多数目，是 43 只。由中国的马庆华于 2006 年 11 月 7 日，在中国山东省潍坊创造。↓

Youngest world record holder, athletics women
最年轻的世界纪录保持者（女子运动员）

The youngest individual record breaker is Wang Yan (China, b. 9th April 1971) who set a women's 5,000 m walk record at age 14 years 334 days with 21 min 33.8 sec at Ji'an, China, on 9th March 1986.

最年轻的女子世界纪录保持者，是中国的王妍。王妍于 1986 年 3 月 9 日，在中国吉安以 21 分 33.8 秒的成绩，创造了一项女子 5,000 米竞走世界纪录，当时她 14 岁 334 天。

Speed skating, short-track, 1,000 m (women)
1,000 米短道速滑比赛纪录（女子）

1:29.495, Wang Meng (China) Harbin, China, 15th March 2008.

女子 1,000 米短道速滑比赛纪录，是 1 分 29 秒 495。由中国的王濛于 2008 年 3 月 15 日，在中国哈尔滨创造。

Stair climbing by bicycle - most steps
骑自行车爬楼梯的最多级数

The record for most steps climbed by bicycle is 2,008 and was achieved by Zhang Jincheng (China), Xavi Casas (Andorra) and Javier Zapata (Colombia) climbing all 88 floors of the Jin Mao Tower in Shanghai, China, on 31st December 2007.

骑自行车爬楼梯的最多级数，是 2,008 级台阶。由中国温州的张金成、安道尔的夏维和哥伦比亚的萨帕塔创造。三人于 2007 年 12 月 31 日，骑自行车爬楼，登上中国上海 88 层的高楼——金茂大厦。

Speed skating, short-track, 500 m (women)
500 米短道速滑比赛纪录（女子）

42.60 seconds, Wang Meng (China) in Beijing, China, on 29th November 2008.

女子 500 米短道速滑比赛纪录，是 42.60 秒。由中国的王濛于 2008 年 11 月 29 日，在中国北京创造。

Most shuttlecock kicks while skipping rope in one minute
1 分钟内边跳绳边踢毽子的最多踢毽次数

The most shuttlecock kicks while skipping rope in one minute is 69 and was achieved by Liu Yunji (China) on the set of *Zheng Da Zong Yi - Guinness World Records Special* in Beijing, China, on 1st November 2007.

1 分钟内边跳绳边踢毽子的最多踢毽次数，是 69 次。由中国的刘云集于 2007 年 11 月 1 日，在"正大综艺·吉尼斯中国之夜"节目上创造。

Tallest human tower
最高的人梯

The tallest human tower consists of six people standing on top of each others shoulders and was performed by the Fuyong Acrobatic Arts Group of Bao An District (all China) on the set of *Zheng Da Zong Yi - Guinness World Records Special* in Beijing, China, on 18th September 2007.

最高的人梯，是人搭成的6层。该纪录由中国深圳宝安区福永杂技团于2007年9月18日，在"正大综艺·吉尼斯中国之夜"节目上创造。←↓

Tallest column of dice
叠单排骰子的
最多层数

The tallest dice column consists of 25 dice and was achieved by Hu Hairong (China) on the set of *Zheng Da Zong Yi - Guinness World Records Special* in Beijing, China, on 14th November 2008.

　　叠单排骰子的最多层数，是 25 层。由中国的胡海荣于 2008 年 11 月 14 日，在"正大综艺·吉尼斯中国之夜"节目上创造。→

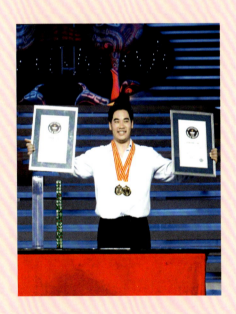

Tallest double column of dice
叠双排骰子的最多层数

The tallest dice double column consists of 42 dice and was achieved by Hu Hairong (China) on the set of *Zheng Da Zong Yi - Guinness World Records Special* in Beijing, China, on 14th November 2008.

　　叠双排骰子的最多层数，是 42 个骰子叠放的。由中国的胡海荣于 2008 年 11 月 14 日，在"正大综艺·吉尼斯中国之夜"节目上创造。←

Youngest person to win a pro beach volleyball title
赢得职业沙滩排球赛冠军的
最年轻球员

At age 17 years 99 days, Xue Chen (China, b. 18th February 1989) became the youngest player to win an international beach volleyball title, the China Shanghai Jinshan Open, in Shanghai, China, on 28th May 2006.

　　赢得职业沙滩排球赛冠军的最年轻球员，是中国的薛晨。2006 年 5 月 28 日，薛晨在世界职业沙滩排球巡回赛中国上海金山公开赛上赢得冠军，当时他 17 岁 99 天。

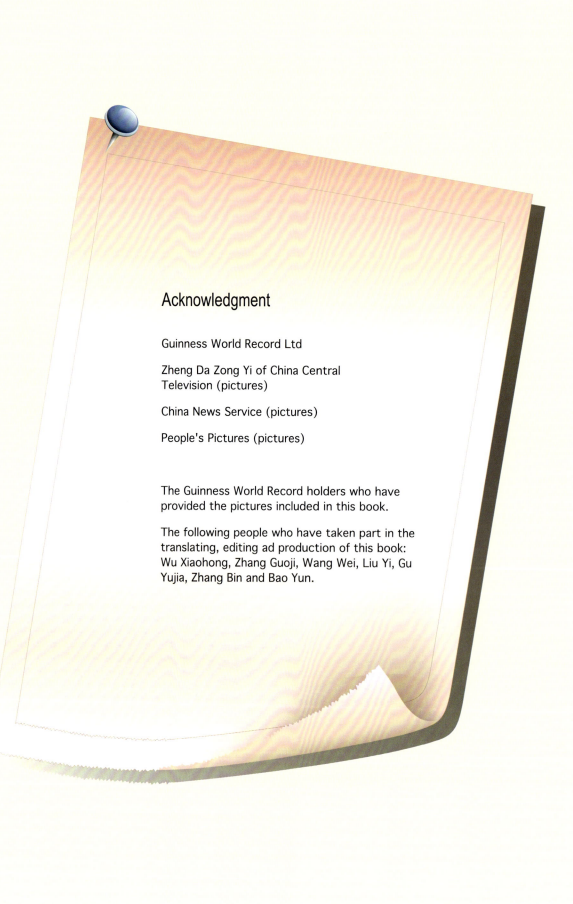

Acknowledgment

Guinness World Record Ltd

Zheng Da Zong Yi of China Central Television (pictures)

China News Service (pictures)

People's Pictures (pictures)

The Guinness World Record holders who have provided the pictures included in this book.

The following people who have taken part in the translating, editing ad production of this book: Wu Xiaohong, Zhang Guoji, Wang Wei, Liu Yi, Gu Yujia, Zhang Bin and Bao Yun.

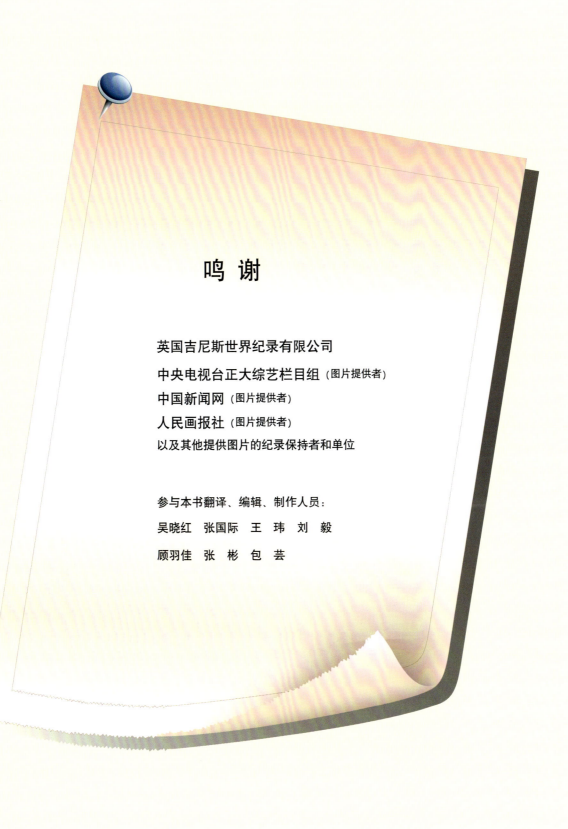

鸣 谢

英国吉尼斯世界纪录有限公司

中央电视台正大综艺栏目组 (图片提供者)

中国新闻网 (图片提供者)

人民画报社 (图片提供者)

以及其他提供图片的纪录保持者和单位

参与本书翻译、编辑、制作人员：

吴晓红　张国际　王　玮　刘　毅

顾羽佳　张　彬　包　芸

本书图片拍摄者（按照片提供顺序）

庐山电影院	王　辉	摄
和谐奥运	吕建设	摄
乐山大佛	张燕军	摄
青藏铁路边的藏羚羊	裴竟德	摄
巨型娃娃鱼	平　白	摄
上海环球金融中心101层世界最高观光厅	海　牛	摄
杨利伟自主出舱后向工作人员挥手致意	孙　阳	摄
天安门广场	邹　宪	摄
上海卢浦大桥	井　韦	摄
长江三峡	梁　斌	摄
美丽的香港	李　刚	摄
雅鲁藏布江的另一面	税晓洁	摄
香港青马大桥	田　地	摄
世界上最长寿的亚洲象林旺	中国新闻网	
磁悬浮列车	钮一新	摄
世界第一跨海大桥——杭州湾跨海大桥	柴燕菲	摄
京杭大运河山东枣庄段	高启民	摄
应县木塔	张长江	摄
王军霞	中国专题图库	
空中看秦始皇陵	中国专题图库	
甘肃敦煌鸣沙山	刘文敏	摄
颐和园长廊	宋学广	摄
长城	姜景余	摄
小寨天坑	赵贵林	摄
神山冈仁波齐	刘志东	摄
鸟瞰故宫全貌	胡敦志	摄
三峡大坝	杜华举	摄
黄河断流	邹　毅	摄
绒布寺	安　然	摄
台北101大楼	中国台湾网